Black-Eyed Susans

CLASSIC STORIES BY AND ABOUT BLACK WOMEN

MARY HELEN WASHINGTON is assistant professor of black literature and the Director of the Center for Black Studies at the University of Detroit. She has contributed essays and criticism to many publications. She received the Richard Wright Award for Literary Criticism from *Black World*, January 1974.

Black-Eyed Susans

CLASSIC STORIES BY AND ABOUT BLACK WOMEN

Edited and with an Introduction
by Mary Helen Washington

Anchor Books
Anchor Press/Doubleday
Garden City, New York

The Anchor Books edition is the first publication of *Black-Eyed Susans: Classic Stories by and About Black Women*
Anchor Books Edition: 1975

Library of Congress Cataloging in Publication Data
Main entry under title:

Black-eyed Susans.

   Bibliography.
   1. Short stories, American—Afro-American authors. 2. Women's writings, American. I. Washington, Mary Helen.
PZ1.B548 [PS647.N35]   813'.01

ISBN: 0-385-09043-9
Library of Congress Catalog Card Number 75-6169

Grateful acknowledgment is made to the following contributors for permission to reprint the material contained within this anthology:

Jean Wheeler Smith for "Frankie Mae," which appeared in *Black World*, 1968. Reprinted by permission of the author.
Toni Morrison for "The Coming of Maureen Peal" and "SEE-MOTHERMOTHERISVERYNICE," which appeared in *The Bluest Eye* (Holt, Rinehart & Winston). Reprinted by permission of Holt, Rinehart & Winston, Publishers. Copyright ©1970 by Toni Morrison.
Gwendolyn Brooks for "The Self-Solace" and "If You're Light and Have Long Hair," which appeared in *Maud Martha* (Harper & Brothers). Reprinted by permission of Harper & Row Publishers, Inc. Copyright © 1953 by Gwendolyn Brooks.
Louise Meriwether for "A Happening in Barbados," which appeared in *The Antioch Review*, 1968. Reprinted by permission of the author.
Toni Cade Bambara for "My Man Bovanne," which appeared in *Gorilla, My Love* (Random House).
Paule Marshall for "Reena," which appeared in *American Negro Short Stories*. Reprinted by permission of the author.
Alice Walker for "Everyday Use," which appeared in *In Love and Trouble* (Harcourt Brace Jovanovich). Copyright © 1973 by Alice Walker. And "A Sudden Trip Home in the Spring," which appeared in *Essence*, 1971. Reprinted by permission of the author. Copyright © 1971 by Alice Walker.

Contents

To the fine black women who brought me up:

Melissa Dalton
Bessie Riffe
Cora Riley
Elsie Wilkins
Sarah Mitchell
Helen Brinson

and most of all to

Mary Catherine Washington

De nigger woman is de mule uh de world so
fur as Ah can see.
Nannie, in ZORA NEALE HURSTON's
Their Eyes Were Watching God

And she had nothing to fall back on:
not maleness, not whiteness, not ladyhood,
not anything. And out of the profound
desolation of her reality, she may very
well have invented herself.
TONI MORRISON

Black-eyed Susan:
"A slight, pretty flower that grows
on any ground; and flowers pledge no
allegiance to banners of any man."
ALICE WALKER

Introduction.

Stereotypes about black women abound like weeds in this society. It is common practice to make slick, easy generalizations about them. Statements such as, black women have always been strong, they've always been liberated, they're treated better than black men, they're evil, they're loud—are made so frequently that they are accepted as known fact. The white media have been in on the act for a long time, of course, creating such perverted fantasies as Beulah, Sapphire, Pinky, and Aunt Jemima, which are adequate evidence of the abuse of the black woman's image. And the habit still persists. People other than the black woman herself try to define who she is, what she is supposed to look like, act like, and sound like. And most of these creations bear very little resemblance to real, live black women.

One of the factors contributing to the misconceptions and confusions surrounding the black woman is the treatment of the black woman writer. Like all black writers, black women have never been fairly represented in anthologies—black or white. They are almost never as well known as Ellison, Wright, Baldwin, or Baraka, not to mention white American authors. It is incredible that major black women novelists such as Toni Morrison, Nella Larsen, Zora Neale Hurston, Gwendolyn Brooks, Dorothy West, Ann Petry, Paule Marshall, Alice Walker, and Margaret Walker are almost never taught in college-level American literature courses and rarely mentioned in women's-studies courses. We are not bemoaning the issue simply because of lack of equal time, but because so many countless generations of men and women have been deprived of the insight and sensitivity of these writers.

What is most important about the black woman writer is her special and unique vision of the black woman. Since *Iola Leroy*, the first novel written by a black woman, published in 1862, one of the main preoccupations of the black woman writer has been the black woman herself—her aspirations, her conflicts, her relationship to her men and her children, her creativity. The black woman writer has looked at the black woman from an insider's point of view and tried to discover what happened to the black woman as she raised a family under ghetto conditions, or as a dayworker in some white woman's kitchen, or as she lived with a man struggling with his own sense of powerlessness, or as she looked into the mirror and tried to see beauty in full features and dark skin. That these writers have firsthand knowledge of their subject ought to be enough to command attention and respect.

This, then, became the focus of this collection: the black woman as seen from the special angle of the black woman writer. Is she any different from the images projected in the media, or by white writers, or by black male writers? What is her childhood like? Is the middle-class black woman merely an imitation white woman? Have her experiences of discrimination been any different from the black man's?

One careful look at any of the stories in this anthology will tell you immediately what the black woman is *not* like. She does not favor in the least the black women created by southern white writers, including Faulkner's Dilsey. Nor is she like any of the current caricatures of the black female on television or in the movies. She cer-

tainly does not fit that legendary and romanticized image
of the black superwoman: long of arm, strong of back,
bold of mouth—in a word, indestructible. One does not
see in the black woman as portrayed by the black woman
writer any such perversions as the super sex object, or
the domineering matriarch, or the evil black bitch.

We are, in fact, in for quite a revelation in the country
of the black woman writer, for the territory is still wilderness. Consider Zora Neale Hurston, a major novelist of
the 1930s, who wrote what is probably the most beautiful
love story of a black man and woman in literature. In this
novel, *Their Eyes Were Watching God* (1937), an old
grandmother, a former slave bought and sold like a bag of
rice and forced to raise a granddaughter in the white folks'
back yard, accurately sums up her position in this society:
"De nigger woman is de mule uh de world so fur as Ah
can see." Not a woman with power, not a liberated
woman (if liberation means the freedom to make choices
about one's life), but a mule, picking up the burdens that
everyone else has thrown down and refused to carry. And
yet another revelation: Consider Alice Walker's startling claim that black women have for centuries been
suppressed artists, some "driven to a numb and bleeding
madness by the springs of creativity in them for which
there was no release."[1] Some of these hidden artists were
driven crazy, but others found a simple way to express
that creativity in such things as quilting, or cooking, or
growing flowers—the activities black women have
watched their mothers and grandmothers engaged in for
years without knowing that true artists were at work.
Toni Morrison's Sula is a hidden artist, but, denied the
means of releasing her artistry, she becomes a destructive

1. Alice Walker, "In Search of Our Mothers' Gardens: The
Creativity of Black Women in the South," *Ms.*, May 1974.

force, restless and bored, sleeping with other people's husbands, defying everybody in her way:

> Had she paints, or clay, or knew the discipline of the dance, or strings; had she anything to engage her tremendous curiosity and her gift for metaphor, she might have exchanged the restlessness and preoccupation with whim for an activity that provided her with all she yearned for. And like any artist with no art form, she became dangerous.

Like Sula, Morrison's Pauline Breedlove, in *The Bluest Eye,* is also an artist but, again, one without an art form until she discovers a grotesque way to express herself—by arranging things in the kitchen of the white woman she works for. Consider the black woman as artist, yearning for creation, needing form to express herself. Imagine what has been lost and destroyed: two centuries of women who would have painted, or sculptured, or modeled clay, or danced, or written stories.

Many of the stories in this collection look backward at the past because we believe it is necessary to understand the past in order to go forward, and there has, as yet, been no adequate investigation of the black woman's past. But there are also stories here that explore the lives of women who provide examples of where it is possible for black women to move. Room to move. A place to move into. A reason to move. This anthology hopes to be part of the process of providing a larger space for black women.

This collection presents many themes dealing with the condition of being black and woman in America: the conflicting relationships between mothers and daughters, the alienation between black women and white women, growing up black and female (a subject that has been given far less attention than the growing up of black boys), the antagonisms between black women and black men, and the intimidation of black women by the American standards of physical beauty. There is a very definite plan in the progression of the stories in this book: it begins with the brutal and unnecessary tragedy of "Frankie Mae" and ends with the hope and promise of "A Sudden Trip Home in the Spring."

GROWING UP BLACK AND FEMALE

Growing up black and female is a subject that has been written about by many of the major black women writers: Toni Morrison's *The Bluest Eye*, Maya Angelou's *I Know Why the Caged Bird Sings*, Louise Meriwether's *Daddy Was a Number Runner*, Paule Marshall's *Brown Girl, Brownstones*, all deal with that subject. As we investigate these stories, certain recurring patterns emerge that tell us a great deal about the uniqueness of the adolescence of the black girl. Almost without exception, these writers describe the black girl's growing up period as essentially unprotected. They show the black girl developing self-reliance and resilience in order to deal with the hostile forces around her, quite often assuming adulthood earlier than she should have to because of the external pressures around her.

These same patterns are evident in Jean Smith's story "Frankie Mae." Frankie learns early how to handle the harsh environment she lives in. By the time she is seven or eight, she knows how to lie to the man who comes to repossess their stove. Working in the cotton fields before she is thirteen, Frankie begins to look, to her father, like a little old woman. When she is fifteen, and in the fourth grade, she has her first child—and three more in the next four years.

It is interesting to see how literature confirms and validates (or rejects) the findings of sociology. In Frankie Mae, Jean Smith has created a character whose life conforms in almost every detail to what Joyce Ladner concluded about the childhood of the black female in her study *Tomorrow's Tomorrow*. Ladner says the lives of black girls in poor environments are characterized by early exposure to violence and to other harsh social forces which parents are unable to protect them from. In spite of these conditions, Ladner has discovered that these black girls develop resources that enable them to protect themselves in some ways, and she finds that they exhibit an unusual degree of emotional stability and strength.

It is startling to see in Frankie Mae such a perfect example of Ladner's observations. This rugged little womanchild, like many of her counterparts in northern urban ghettoes, has a maturity and self-reliance far beyond her years. She possesses amazing coping strategies for absorbing disappointments and pain. But, finally, overwhelmed by forces larger than herself, she also knows defeat.

Several details in this story suggest that "Frankie Mae" is meant to have the force of a parable. The father, for instance, is a man named Brown; he works on the Whites' Plantation for a man named Mr. White, Junior. The time is the early sixties. Brown is the timekeeper for the place, and when he hands over the timekeeper's watch at the end of the story and joins the boycott against White, he is signaling an end to the old order and the beginning of a new era for black people. The life of Frankie Mae is also symbolic. Frankie could be any of the millions of girls who were poor and black in the South before the civil rights movement. It is her suffering (and theirs) that supplies the courage for someone to stand up and fight back.

THE INTIMIDATION OF COLOR

The subject of the black woman's physical beauty occurs with such frequency in the writing of black women that it indicates they have been deeply affected by the discrimination against the shade of their skin and the texture of their hair. In almost every novel or autobiography written by a black woman, there is at least one incident in which the dark-skinned girl wishes to be either white or light-skinned with "good" hair. Often the child experiences this desire with frightening intensity. Maya Angelou says in her autobiography, *I Know Why the Caged Bird Sings*, that her fantasy as a child was to wake out of her black, ugly dream and surprise everyone when they discovered that she really had blond hair and blue eyes and had been turned into an ugly black girl by her cruel stepmother. In her autobiographical statement *Report from Part One*, Gwen Brooks relates the experiences of being a dark-skinned child, which implied being of less worth than a "high-yellow" child. It never occurred to her that black skin would someday be thought beautiful. She simply learned early and well that being acceptable meant being "Bright," having hair of "Good Grade," not "Hot Comb Straight." Since she had neither, she took her place among the "Lesser Blacks," a status that was confirmed by the little boys at school who rechristened her "Ol' Black Gal."

Besides Shirley Temple movies, white-baby dolls, and other little black kids, what really convinced the black girl that she was truly undesirable was the reaction of adults to a "high-yellow" child. That child was cooed over, boasted about, clucked approvingly at, and received gentle and affectionate treatment from the world of "Big People." The classic example of this phenomenon is Maureen Peal, from Toni Morrison's *The Bluest Eye*. A "high-yellow dream child," Maureen intrudes into the lives of Claudia and Frieda, the two "ordinary"-looking black girls, spreading a bone-deep chill. When Maureen screams at them that she is cute and that they are black

and ugly, they are not able to deny the truth of that statement, because it has been so convincingly validated by
those with the authority to do so:

> Dolls we could destroy, but we could not destroy the
> honey voices of parents and aunts, the obedience in
> the eyes of our peers, the slippery light in the eyes of
> our teachers when they encountered the Maureen
> Peals of the world. . . . And all the time we knew
> that Maureen Peal was not the Enemy and not
> worthy of such intense hatred. The *Thing* to fear
> was the *Thing* that made *her* beautiful, and not us.

The early lessons of beauty were religiously passed on
to the adult black woman, sometimes wordlessly. The rav-
ing beauties every high school boy coveted were invariably light-skinned with "good" hair. Sometimes these lessons came across with the conviction of a commandment:
Marry someone to lighten up your family; don't wear light
colors, they make dark skin look blacker. The ultimate sin
was not to care enough to fight it, but even the determined fight made one only acceptable, not beautiful. In
Gwen Brooks's novel *Maud Martha* (1953), Maryginia
Washington, one of the roomers in Maud Martha's building, advises her darker sister to apply lightening creams to
her skin, because

> they ain't no sense in lookin' any worse'n you have
> to, is they, dearie?

In other words, the goal for the dark woman is not even
beauty. The "ideal" is completely out of the question. The
goal is not true beauty, but to be passable, not to be offensive.

When Maud Martha goes to the Foxy Cats Ball in the
story "If You're Light and Have Long Hair," her husband, Paul, sits her on a bench by the wall and goes to
dance with a stranger who is "red-haired and curved, and

white as white." The attention Paul gives this stranger makes Maud immediately aware of "the color thing" that she and Paul have never been able to lick:

> What I am inside, what is really me, he likes okay. But he keeps looking at my color, which is like a wall. He has to jump over it in order to meet and touch what I've got for him. He has to jump away up high in order to see it. He gets awful tired of all that jumping.

At first, Maud thinks of confronting the woman. But then she realizes that would be like hacking away at a leaf on a dying tree. What is wrong is the way Paul and Maud feel about themselves and each other, as though their color had devalued them.

If the stories of these writers are to be believed, then the color/hair problem has cut deep into the psyche of the black woman. It is that particular aspect of oppression that has affected, for the most part, only women. I could not find a single piece of fiction written by a black male in which he feels ugly or rejected because of the shade of his skin or the texture of his hair. In contrast, the color theme almost always plays at least a peripheral role—more often a significant one—in the lives of the women characters created by women writers. Toni Morrison says in *The Bluest Eye* that the concept of physical beauty is one of the most destructive ideas in the history of human thought. We can see it taken to its most violent extreme in the life of Morrison's Pecola, who wishes for blue eyes as a sign of grace. In a world where she is considered unforgivably ugly, Pecola redeems herself by imagining that she has the bluest eyes of all and that those eyes make her invulnerable to the attacks against her. Safe behind those blue eyes, she quietly goes mad. But even in less violent terms, the idea of beauty as defined by white America has been an assault on the personhood of the black woman.

THE BLACK WOMAN AND THE MYTH OF THE WHITE WOMAN

June Jordan's poem *What Would I Do White?* is one black woman's view of what it is like to be a white woman. In that poem, white women are depicted as rich, haughty, lazy, and acquisitive. Trying to imagine what she would do if she were white, the poet concludes

> I would do nothing
> That would be enough.

That implies, of course, the worthlessness of white women's lives. The hostility expressed in this poem is often found in the black woman writer's attitude toward white women. The white woman as she appears in the literature of black women is almost always described in negative terms: a callous and indifferent employer of black domestics, a phony liberal, a southern racist participating with her men in a lynching, the snobbish upper-class woman. And without exception, she is always condescending to the black woman.

Though the two stories "The Self-Solace" and "A Happening in Barbados" deal ostensibly with the antagonisms and hostilities between the black woman and the white woman, they are more concerned with the complexities behind the black woman's response to the white woman. It is significant that the white women in both stories are unwitting agents, unintentionally provoking situations that unleash the scorn, pity, or anger of the black women. The white saleswoman in "The Self-Solace," for example, casually uses the word "nigger" in the course of conversation, totally unaware that she has said anything offensive. That is not so surprising as the fact that neither of the two black women confronts her; in fact, they both deny the reality of the remark and its effect on them and offer several rationalizations for not speaking up. Maud Martha pretends not to hear it, and Sonia Johnson claims she is unaffected by racial slurs, she herself not being a nigger. We, however, know by all their psychological squirmings and inner tension over the remark that they are very much intimidated by the woman, by her whiteness, and by the power the word has over them.

In Louise Meriwether's "A Happening in Barbados" the white woman, Glenda, is similarly unaware of the effect of her actions, so the attention of this story is also focused on the inner conflict of the black woman. The beautiful and sophisticated narrator (she remains unnamed) gives evidence early in the story of a generalized hostility for white women. At first her reactions to Glenda are stereotypical: white women, she says, are always trying to snatch black men. The worst ones, like Glenda, want to imitate blacks. All of them are pampered, spoiled, and essentially weak women who have been taken care of all their lives. At the first opportunity, the black woman takes her revenge—and in the most devastating way possible; but in the process of exacting revenge, the narrator is forced to lay bare her own soul, and we see beneath the tough and bitter exterior. The act of revenge causes a shattering revelation for the narrator. She sees that out of her own bitterness she has been callous and vicious, using the woman's white skin as an excuse to justify her own inhumanity.

The black women in both of these stories are forced to confront their feelings about white women. In neither case are the black women reacting to an individual white woman. They are reacting to centuries of abuse, alienation, and hostility, in short to what White Woman has meant to Black Woman. They are reacting to the privileged status of white women in this country; they are reacting to all the years that black women have done slave work and daywork in the homes of white women while neglecting their own; to all those white women who called them by their first names no matter how old they were, while they continued to address their employer as Mrs. So-and-So; to all the times white women were given jobs up front in the store while they were stuck back in the stock room or in the kitchen, where they would not be seen; to all the years when it was possible for a white woman to pretend rape and have a black man executed and no one to whom a black woman could cry rape. The inequities are legion and could be catalogued *ad infinitum*, but that is not necessary, since the abuses are all-too-well known and all-too-deeply felt.

Given the fact that the white woman still enjoys more privileged and protected status than the black woman, it is no surprise that the relationship between them is still tied to the past. Because of that past, it is a painful and conflicting task for the black woman to probe her feelings in this area. One senses that conflict when black women are asked to respond to "Women's Lib." Certainly black women recognize that they have some of the same problems as white women, particularly in employment. But racial oppression points up the essential separateness of white and black women. Not only have white women participated in the racist structure of this country, but black women have been devalued because they were judged inferior to the "ideal" white woman. In view of these facts, the courage and honesty of the black women writers who have dared to confront such a highly emotional subject are all the more impressive.

The Black Mother-Daughter Conflict

The black mother frequently appears in literature as a figure of towering strength. She is fiercely protective of her children, often sacrificing herself to prepare them to live in a violent and racist world. The prototype of the noble black mother is Lena Younger, in Lorraine Hansberry's *Raisin in the Sun*. Mama Younger runs a household, including a grown daughter and a grown son and his wife, with absolute religious convictions and an iron hand. In spite of her children's failings, Lena is unsparing of herself where they are concerned. She never loses faith in God, in herself, or in her family. She is, in a word, invincible, a larger-than-life figure, perhaps even a stereotype. Looking over the stories that black women have written about their mothers and grandmothers, I am impressed with the frequency of this image: the powerful black mother. Black writers depict the black mother as a woman faced with harsh responsibilities which she accepts and carries out to the fullest of her powers. Of course, this is history. Black women have seen their mothers and aunts and grandmothers taking care of their families under the most severe circumstances. What Angela Davis said of the black slave woman also applies for many generations afterward:

> . . . the alleged benefits of the ideology of femininity did not accrue to her. She was not sheltered or protected; she would not remain oblivious to the desperate struggle for existence unfolding outside the "home." She was also there in the fields, alongside the man, toiling under the lash from sun-up to sundown.[2]

The black woman was not permitted the dubious distinction of being feminine. She was not sheltered or protected or exempted from hard work or the lash. She toiled beside her man in the struggle for existence. That is the tradition the black woman comes from.

2. Angela Davis, "Reflections on the Black Woman's Role in the Community of Slaves," *The Black Scholar*, Vol. 3, No. 3, December 1971, p. 7.

And yet I still maintain in the face of these hard facts that tradition is no excuse for cliché. And I think the image of the strong, unfaltering black mother has tended to become a cliché. Mama Younger, to use one example, belongs to this tradition, and her characterization lacks the dimension necessary to make her a complex, real, live woman. On the other hand, Eva Peace, in Toni Morrison's *Sula*, is not the monolithic, strong black woman but a strange and complicated woman whose very strength is a part of the mask she wears to keep herself and her family intact. When Eva's grown daughter Hannah asks her mother if she loved her three children, Eva's plain, hostile answer is, "No. I don't reckon I did. Not the way you thinkin'," and she accuses Hannah of thinking evil for even asking such a question. Later, she feels the need to explain that "No," but the rest of her answer is so brutal that the love behind it is almost unrecognizable:

> . . . what you talkin' 'bout did I love you girl. I stayed alive for you can't you get that through your thick head or what is that between your ears heifer?

This is the love of a woman who battled her way through life in order to keep her kids from starving at a time when "Niggers was dying like flies." When it would have been easier to die or run off; she simply stayed alive for them. She did not have anything left over to play around with them or teach them games or be silly with them and so her strength actually seems like a kind of cold indifference. That very same day, however, Eva, a one-legged woman, hurls herself out of a second-story window in an attempt to save Hannah's life. What saves Eva (and Hannah) from being stereotyped strong black mothers is ambiguity. They are never entirely what we expect. Eva takes care of her children, but she does so without physical affection or tenderness. When she discovers her son is a junkie, she burns him to death, because she cannot allow his self-destruction. Her granddaughter, Sula, is so frightened of her that she has Eva put away; Eva is seen finally as a senile, paranoid old woman, rotting away in an asylum. Eva is one of the most complex black mothers in literature. Because she cannot be easily explained or neatly categorized, she defies the stereotype.

The two mothers in the mother-daughter section of this anthology are not neat little clichés either. Hazel Lee Peoples, in Toni Bambara's story "My Man Bovanne" is a wig-wearing, hip-shaking, good-time woman who causes her children much embarrassment and concern because she refuses to conform to their more militant ideals. And Mama, in Alice Walker's "Everyday Use," is carefully drawn to show that underneath her apparent personal strength, she is unnerved by the conflict with her daughter Dee. In both stories, the problems between black mother and daughter are caused by the conflict between the militant values of the younger generation and the more conservative, traditional values of the parents. Elo, the daughter in "My Man Bovanne," tries to browbeat her mother, Hazel Peoples, into wearing African clothes and hair style, but Hazel is insulted by the smug self-righteousness of Elo's nationalism and remembers when her daughter refused to wear her hair cornrowed because it looked "country." The daughter, Dee, in "Everyday Use" also considers herself something of a black cultural nationalist. With a newly acquired African name and an African-looking wardrobe, she criticizes her mother's "non-revolutionary" ways. Both Dee and Elo, having grown distant from the "grass roots" life-styles of their past and condescending toward that past, are intimidating women. Neither of the mothers in these two stories is quite sure how things have deteriorated to the point where they must be criticized for who they are, but, with a certainness about their own identities, they maintain their ground.

Tracing the historical roots of this conflict between black mothers and daughters, we can go all the way back to Zora Hurston's *Their Eyes Were Watching God* (published in 1937) and find early evidence of such conflict in the quarrels between Nannie and her daughter, Leafy, and then her granddaughter, Janie. It is essentially the same conflict that is evident between Judy and Cleo in Dorothy West's *The Living Is Easy*, published in 1948, and between Beneatha and Mama in Hansberry's *Raisin in the Sun* (1959), and between Silla and Selina in Paule Marshall's *Brown Girl, Brownstones* (1959). The conflict is basically between the idealists (the daughters) and the pragmatists (the mothers and/or grandmothers). We see the mothers in these conflicts as the ones whose lives are spent struggling for the necessities—food, or clothing, or a place for their children to live, or an education for them, or a good marriage. Like Zora Hurston's character Nannie, they want their children "to pick from a higher bush and a sweeter berry," and they are grieved to see their children making choices that they do not understand, turning their backs on the things the mothers have struggled a lifetime to attain.

In a poem by Carolyn Rodgers dealing with the conflicts between her and her mother, Ms. Rodgers points out that she came to terms with her mother when she realized the truth of that Gullah proverb "Never 'spise de bridge dat carry you safely ober." As the words of that old proverb suggest, her mother was just such a bridge—one that had carried her safely over. Such a reconciliation also takes place between Silla and Selina in Marshall's *Brown Girl, Brownstones* when the daughter, Selina, recognizes and accepts the kinship that has always existed between her and her mother. The recognition of their kinship is the beginning for Selina of forging an identity for herself, an identity that emerges as she comes to know and understand and accept her own past.

There seems to be a clear message in these stories about conflicts between black mother and daughter. The conflict is not only personal but historical. And the resolution of the conflict can be discovered only as one comes to terms with history.

THE BLACK WOMAN AND THE DISAPPOINTMENT OF ROMANTIC LOVE

If the stories and poems written by black women are any indication, then black women have had more than their share of trouble in love. Following the myth of romantic love, they too have sometimes watched their dreams narrowed down to a few bitter choices. Two stories that deal with the promise and disappointment of love are Paule Marshall's "Reena," and Toni Morrison's "SEEMOTHERMOTHERISVERYNICE" from her novel *The Bluest Eye*. The two women in these selections —Reena and Pauline Breedlove—are from totally different backgrounds: Reena's family is urban and aspiring middle class; Pauline's is rural and poor. Yet some of the same "inconditions of love" are present in both lives.

For Pauline Breedlove, marriage *is* the Great Happening in her life. A young woman with a crippled foot, Pauline is grateful for the love of Cholly Breedlove. She marries him and moves North, expecting her dreams of romantic love and a better life to be fulfilled. Instead she finds in the northern urban ghetto loneliness and poverty and the chronic conflicts between husband and wife that accompany them. Finally, on top of everything else, Pauline discovers through the movies a realization of her own ugliness and the ugliness of her life. In the picture show, she sees the other side—the "ideal" way to live—and she knows how far her life is from that ideal. At the movies she sees

> White men taking such care of they women, and they all dressed up in a big clean house with the bathtubs right in the same room with the toilet. Them pictures gave me a lot of pleasure, but it made coming home hard, and looking at Cholly hard.

And so when she comes home to Cholly, they fight. And they fight with a premeditated passion. Pauline fights Cholly because he cannot provide her with what she gets in the white folks' kitchen. And Cholly fights her for the look on her face that says he has failed her.

The story of Reena and her man is different from Pauline's only because Reena is not a poor and uneducated domestic worker. Her life is strikingly similar, however, to many black middle-class women. The patterns are easily recognizable: the theme of her childhood was being too dark-skinned to please the little light-skinned boys of her youth. Then, in college, she becomes involved in all the serious causes to protest injustices. She changes her hair to Afro and has her first interracial affair, which ends badly. After college she, like many black women, is unable to find a job in her field, so she joins the Welfare Department as an investigator. And like any number of unmarried professional black women in any of the big cities—New York, Los Angeles, Washington, Detroit—her life follows a predictable sequence:

> . . . the job teaching or doing social work . . . the small apartment with kitchenette which they sometimes shared with a roommate; a car, some of them; membership in various political and social action organizations for the militant few like Reena; the vacations in Mexico, Europe, the West Indies, and now Africa; the occasional date. . . . Alone and lonely, and indulging themselves while they wait.

In this account of the previous twenty years of her life, the most painful part is her marriage. Reena marries a professional photographer, and so as not to threaten him, she tries to fit into the roles of woman-behind-her-man, devoted mother, and submissive housewife. But her husband's career in photography is disappointing to him: "Dave also wanted the big, gaudy, commercial success that would dazzle and confound that white world downtown and force it to *see* him." Again the old problem of definitions. It is the white world's definition of himself that he must live up to. When Reena begins to work again, her husband sees it as her way of pointing up his deficiencies, and he accuses Reena of wanting to see him fail. Not able to live with the anger and despair that creeps into their marriage, they are divorced.

After the divorce, Reena's earlier spirit of independence emerges. A successful and capable journalist, active again in social causes, she begins to plan a future for herself that includes living and working in Africa, where her children will have a chance to see black people with a place and a history and an identity of their own. There will be no white dolls for them, she declares.

All along, Reena's story has been deeply involved with the black woman's history. Three generations of black women are represented in the story: Aunt Vi, who is being buried, lived out her life "sleeping in" at white folks' houses with "Thursdays and every other Sunday off"; Reena and Paulie, who, in confronting the past, have lived out the last cycle of closed off, dead-end, and frustrated lives; and Reena's children, who are the beneficiaries of the struggles of the past generations. Two of the central themes in Paule Marshall's work—the importance of confronting the past, both in personal and historical terms, and the necessity of reversing the present order—are brought together in this story.[3] This is what really makes Reena's story different from Pauline's. Reena is able to confront the past because of her awareness of herself, her understanding of the political and economic oppressions that underlie her condition, and because she has the power—economic, political, and personal—to move to change things for herself and her children. With the authority that comes from her unsparing honesty, Reena makes clear that the old fantasies and old definitions limiting and constricting the black woman cannot and will not be continued.

But neither of these two stories offers any new definitions for relationships between black women and black men in the future. These two stories and many other stories black women have written about love and marriage suggest that relationships between black men and black women are often deadlocked. In the past there was much fighting and knocking of heads (the woman's, usually), these antagonisms being brought on, for the most part, because of the economic and political powerlessness of the black family. The literature of black women strongly implies that in the future the black woman will more and more choose to be alone. Look at the evidence. At the end of nearly all the short stories and novels written by black women in the seventies, the major female character is without a man: Sula and Nel in Toni Morrison's *Sula*, Pauline in Morrison's *The Bluest Eye*, Mrs. Coffin in Louise Meriwether's *Daddy Was a Number Runner*, Lonnie in Meriwether's "That Girl from Creektown," Merle Kibona in Paule Marshall's *The Chosen Place, the Timeless People*, both Silla and Selina in Marshall's *Brown Girl, Brownstones*. The pattern of a woman left

3. Paule Marshall, "Shaping the World of My Art," in *New Letters*, Autumn 1973, p. 111.

without a man, so clearly evident, is perhaps unconscious. Nevertheless it is a powerful statement. The literature of black women provides only a few images of the black man and woman surviving together: Margaret Walker's *Jubilee* (1966), Lorraine Hansberry's *Raisin in the Sun* (1959), and Zora Neale Hurston's *Their Eyes Were Watching God* (1937) are depictions of black love affairs in which there is growth for both individuals and continued commitment to each other. They are not idealized love stories, but they do show the possibility of black men and women staying together.

RECONCILIATION

Alice Walker's "A Sudden Trip Home in the Spring" is also about what is possible. It shows the reconciliation between black men and black women and also a reconciliation between the past and the present. In Sarah Davis, the main character of that story, we have a witness to the end of the old cycle of confusion and despair and alienation. Sarah represents the woman whose newly found consciousness, rather than alienating her from her roots, makes her more aware of the necessity of keeping alive in herself a sense of continuity with the past and a sense of community with her family.

Going home to bury her father, Sarah begins the process of reconciliation. In the past, she has seen her father as she sees all black men—with defeat in his face. Standing alone before his casket, she reassesses her father's life, facing the truth that she has denied him without ever trying to understand his life.

Watching her grandfather take care of the family during the funeral answers another of Sarah's questions. This man is simply and solemnly heroic, holding the family together, never giving in to his own grief. In him Sarah sees a new image of black men, an image that is derived from his relationship to his family, not from the judgment of the white world.

As Sarah's father and grandfather stand for the past, her brother represents the future. He is the militant black man who understands and guards the past while fighting for change—a calm, thoughtful radical. In her metaphor of the family as an ancient house, Sarah pictures her brother as the door to all the other rooms, because he has found a way to connect the past, present, and future.

In the final section of the story (the story is divided into seven sections, each documenting Sarah's movement toward wholeness), Sarah returns to the upper-class college she attends, and the contrast between her own, new sense of herself and the superficial college world is immediately evident. She thinks to herself:

I am a woman in the world. I have buried my father, and shall soon know how to make my grandpa up in stone.

This recognition of her womanhood is the sign that her homecoming has established something about her identity. The reconciliation between Sarah and her father, the discovery of her grandfather's courage and grace, the new closeness with her brother, have allowed her to cast off the old image of black men as defeated.

As she is drawn into more meaningful contact with her own, black world, Sarah experiences a greater disaffinity with the white world, whose values are in conflict with her deepest feelings. One important theme in the writings of black women writers is that aspiring after the white world creates antagonisms among the black community; that, conversely, the deepest and most lasting relationships occur among those black people who are most closely allied with and influenced by their own community. In "A Sudden Trip Home in the Spring," the influence of

the white world is an obstacle to Sarah's personal sense of
liberation and to her creative talent. The sculpture of her
grandfather, signifying a return to her black roots, is one
of the signs of freeing herself.

DIRECTIONS

The authors of the stories in this collection have broken
through the old myths and fantasies about black women.
Their stories are considered classics because, in probing
the black woman's experiences with integrity and skill,
they offer a vision of black women that has dimension
and complexity as well as fidelity to history. And yet there
still remains something of a sacred-cow attitude in regard
to black women that prevents exploration of many aspects
of their lives. In the past, the black woman's image has
been degraded; she herself has been abused both in life
and in literature. It is understandable, therefore, that
there is a desire to protect and revere the black woman's
image. In fact, nowadays any attitude toward the black
woman that falls short of reverence seems to be dis-
loyal. But to write stories with one eye on upholding
the sacredness of black womanhood is to invite manipula-
tion and distortion, when what we need from black writers is insight and honesty. Adopting the attitude of
reverence means that we must settle for some idealized
nonsense about black women and remain deprived of real
characters from whom we could learn more about ourselves.

We need stories, poems, novels, and biographies about
black women who have nervous breakdowns, not just the
ones who endure courageously; stories about women who
are overwhelmed by sex; wives who are not faithful;
women experiencing the pain and humiliation of divorce;
single women over thirty or forty, trying to make sense out
of life and perhaps not being able to; and what about

black women who abuse and neglect their children, or those women whose apparently promiscuous behavior has caused them to be labeled "easy," or those black women in interracial relationships? Until the sacred cow is killed, these stories cannot and will not get told. And I long to read these stories. I need the insight they can give me about real black women.

When I think of how essentially alone black women have been—alone because of our bodies, over which we have had so little control; alone because the damage done to our men has prevented their closeness and protection; and alone because we have had no one to tell us stories about ourselves; I realize that black women writers are an important and comforting presence in my life. Only they know my story. It is absolutely necessary that they be permitted to discover and interpret the entire range and spectrum of the experiences of black women and not be stymied by preconceived conclusions. Because of these writers, there are more models of how it is possible for us to live, there are more choices for black women to make, and there is a larger space in the universe for us.

MARY HELEN WASHINGTON

University of Detroit
Detroit, Michigan
April 9, 1975

Growing Up Black and Female

Frankie Mae

JEAN WHEELER SMITH

The sun had just started coming up when the men gathered at the gate of the White Plantation. They leaned on the fence, waiting. No one was nervous, though. They'd all been waiting a long time. A few more minutes couldn't make much difference. They surveyed the land that they were leaving, the land from which they had brought forth seas of cotton.

Old Man Brown twisted around so that he leaned sideways on the gate. Even though he was in his fifties, he was still a handsome man. Medium-sized, with reddish-brown skin. His beard set him apart from the others; it was the same mixture of black and gray as his hair, but while his hair looked like wool, the strands of his beard were long and nearly straight. He was proud of it, and even when he wasn't able to take a bath, he kept his beard neatly cut and shaped into a V.

He closed his eyes. The sun was getting too bright; it made his headache worse. Damn, he thought, I sure wouldn't be out here this early on no Monday morning if it wasn't for what we got to do today. Whiskey'll sure kill you if you don't get some sleep long with it. I wasn't never just crazy 'bout doing this, anyway. Wonder what made me decide to go along?

Then he smiled to himself. 'Course. It was on account of Frankie Mae. She always getting me into something.

Frankie was his first child, born twenty-two years ago, during the war. When she was little, she had gone everywhere with him. He had a blue bicycle with a rusty wire basket in the front. He used to put Frankie Mae in the basket and ride her to town with him and to the cafe, and sometimes they'd go nowhere special, just riding. She'd sit sideways so that she could see what was on the road ahead and talk with him at the same time. She never bothered to hold onto the basket; she knew her daddy wouldn't let her fall. Frankie fitted so well into the basket that for a few years the Old Man thought that it was growing with her.

She was a black child, with huge green eyes that seemed to glow in the dark. From the age of four on, she had a look of being full-grown. The look was in her muscular, well-defined limbs that seemed like they could do a woman's work and in her way of seeing everything around her. Most times, she was alive and happy. The only thing wrong with her was that she got hurt so easy. The slightest rebuke sent her crying; the least hint of disapproval left her moody and depressed for hours. But on the other side of it was that she had a way of springing back from pain. No matter how hurt she had been, she would be her old self by the next day. The Old Man worried over her. He wanted most to cushion her life.

When Frankie reached six, she became too large to ride in the basket with him. Also, he had four more children by then. So he bought a car for $40. Not long afterward, he became restless. He'd heard about how you could make a lot of money over in the delta. So he decided to go over there. He packed what he could carry in one load—the children, a few chickens, and a mattress—and slipped off one night.

Two days after they left the hills, they drove up to the White Plantation in Leflore County, Mississippi. They were given a two-room house that leaned to one side and five dollars to make some groceries with for the next month.

The Old Man and his wife, Mattie, worked hard that

year. Up at four-thirty and out to the field. Frankie Mae stayed behind to nurse the other children and to watch the pot that was cooking for dinner. At sundown they came back home and got ready for the next day. They did a little sweeping, snapped some beans for dinner the next day, and washed for the baby. Then they sat on the porch together for maybe a half hour.

That was the time the Old Man liked best, the half hour before bed. He and Frankie talked about what had happened during the day, and he assured her that she had done a good job keeping up the house. Then he went on about how smart she was going to be when she started school. It would be in two years, when the oldest boy was big enough to take care of the others.

One evening on the porch Frankie said, "A man from town come by today looking for our stove. You know, the short one, the one ain't got no hair. Said we was three week behind and he was gonna take it. Had a truck to take it back in, too."

The Old Man lowered his head. He was ashamed that Frankie had had to face that man by herself. No telling what he said to her. And she took everything so serious. He'd have to start teaching her how to deal with folks like that.

"What did you tell him, baby?" he asked. "He didn't hurt you none, did he?"

"No, he didn't bother me, sides looking mean. I told him I just this morning seen some money come in the mail from Uncle Ed in Chicago. And I heard my daddy say he was gonna use it to pay off the stove man. So he said, 'Well, I give y'all one more week, one more.' And he left."

The Old Man pulled Frankie to him and hugged her. "You did 'zactly right, honey." She understood. She would be able to take care of herself.

The end of their first year in the delta, the Old Man
and Mattie went to settle up. It was just before Christmas.
When their turn came, they were called by Mr. White
Junior, a short fat man, with a big stomach, whose clothes
were always too tight.

"Let me see, Johnnie," he said. "Here it is. You owe
two hundred dollars."

The Old Man was surprised. Sounded just like he was
back in the hills. He had expected things to be different
over here. He had made a good crop. Should have cleared
something. Well, no sense in arguing. The bossman
counted out fifty dollars.

"Here's you some Christmas money," Mr. White
Junior said. "Pay me when you settle up next year."

The Old Man took the money to town the same day
and bought himself some barrels and some pipes and a
bag of chopped corn. He had made whiskey in the hills,
and he could make it over here, too. You could always find
somebody to buy it. Wasn't no reason he should spend all
his time farming if he couldn't make nothing out of it. He
and Mattie put up their barrels in the trees down by the
river and set their mash to fermentate.

By spring, Brown had a good business going. He sold to
the colored cafes and even to some of the white ones. And
folks knew they could always come to his house if they
ran out. He didn't keep the whiskey at the house, though.
Too dangerous. It was buried down by the water. When
folks came unexpected, it was up to Frankie and her
brother next to her to go get the bottles. Nobody noticed
children. The Old Man bought them a new red wagon for
their job.

He was able to pay off his stove and to give Mattie some
money every once in a while. And they ate a little better
now. But still they didn't have much more than before,
because Brown wasn't the kind of man to save. Also, he

had to do a lot of drinking himself to keep up his sales. Folks didn't like to drink by themselves. When he'd start to drinking, he usually spent up or gave away whatever he had in his pocket. So they still had to work as hard as ever for Mr. White Junior. Brown enjoyed selling the whiskey, though, and Mattie could always go out and sell a few bottles in case of some emergency like their lights being cut off. So they kept the business going.

That spring, Mr. White Junior decided to take them off shares. He would pay $1.50 a day for chopping cotton, and he'd pay by the hundred pound for picking. The hands had no choice. They could work by the day or leave. Actually, the Old Man liked it better working by the day. Then he would have more time to see to his whiskey.

Also, Mr. White Junior made Brown the timekeeper over the other hands. Everybody had drunk liquor with him, and most folks liked him. He did fight too much. But the hands knew that he always carried his pistol. If anybody fought him, they'd have to be trying to kill him, 'cause he'd be trying to kill them.

Brown was given a large, battered watch. So he'd know what time to stop for dinner. His job was to see that the hands made a full day in the field and that all the weeds got chopped. The job was easier than getting out there chopping, in all that sun. So Brown liked it. The only hard part was in keeping after the women whose time was about to come. He hated to see them dragging to the field, their bellies about to burst. They were supposed to keep up with the others, which was impossible. Oftentimes, Mr. White Junior slipped up on the work crew and found one of the big-bellied women lagging behind the others.

"Goddammit, Johnnie," he'd say, "I done told you to keep the hands together. Queenester is way behind. I don't pay good money for folks to be standing around. If she sick, she need to go home."

Sometimes the Old Man felt like defending the woman. She had done the best she could. But then he'd think, No, better leave things like they is.

"You sure right, Mr. White Junior. I was just 'bout to send her home myself. Some niggers too lazy to live."

He would walk slowly across the field to the woman. "I'm sorry, Queenester. The bossman done seen you. I told you all to be looking out for him! Now you got to go. You come back tomorrow, though. He won't hardly be back in this field so soon. I try and let you make two more days this week. I know you need the little change."

The woman would take up her hoe and start walking home. Mr. White Junior didn't carry no hands except to eat dinner and to go home after the day had been made.

One day when he had carried the hands in from the field, Mr. White Junior stopped the Old Man as he was climbing down from the back of the pickup truck. While the bossman talked, Brown fingered his timekeeper's watch that hung on a chain from his belt.

"Johnnie," Mr. White Junior said, "it don't look right to me for you to leave a girl at home that could be working when I need all the hands I can get. And you the time-keeper, too. This cotton can't wait on you all to get ready to chop it. I want Frankie Mae out there tomorrow."

He had tried to resist. "But we getting along with what me and Mattie makes. Ain't got nothing, but we eating. I wants Frankie Mae to go to school. We can do without the few dollars she would make."

"I want my cotton chopped," White said, swinging his fat, sweating body into the truck. "Get that girl down here tomorrow. Don't nobody stay in my house and don't work."

That night the Old Man dreaded the half hour on the

porch. When Frankie had started school that year, she had already been two years late. And she had been so excited about going.

When the wood had been gathered and the children cleaned up, he followed Frankie onto the sloping porch. She fell to telling him about the magnificent yellow bus in which she rode to school. He sat down next to her on the step.

"Frankie Mae, I'm going to tell you something."

"What's that, Daddy? Mama say I been slow 'bout helping 'round the house since I been going to school? I do better. Guess I lost my head."

"No, baby. That ain't it at all. You been helping your mama fine." He stood up to face her but could not bring his eyes to the level of her bright, happy face.

"Mr. White Junior stopped me today when I was getting off the truck. Say he want you to come to field till the chopping get done."

She found his eyes. "What did you say, Daddy?"

"Well, I told him you wanted to go to school, and we could do without your little money. But he say you got to go."

The child's eyes lost their brilliance. Her shoulders slumped, and she began to cry softly. Tired, the Old Man sat back down on the step. He took her hand and sat with her until long after Mattie and the other children had gone to bed.

The next morning, Frankie was up first. She put on two blouses and a dress and some pants to keep off the sun and found herself a rag to tie around her head. Then she woke up her daddy and the others, scolding them for being so slow.

"We got to go get all that cotton chopped! And y'all laying round wasting good daylight. Come on."

Brown got up and threw some water on his face. Here

was Frankie bustling around in her layers of clothes, looking like a little old woman, and he smiled. That's how
Frankie Mae was. She'd feel real bad, terrible, for a few
hours, but she always snapped back. She'd be all right
now.

On the way to the field he said, "Baby, I'm gonna make
you the water girl. All you got to do is carry water over to
them that hollers for it and keep your bucket full. You
don't have to chop none lest you see Mr. White Junior
coming."

"No, Daddy, that's all right. The other hands'll say you
was letting me off easy 'cause I'm yours. Say you taking
advantage of being timekeeper. I go on and chop with the
rest."

He tried to argue with her, but she wouldn't let him
give her the water bucket. Finally, he put her next to Mattie so she could learn from her. As he watched over the
field, he set himself not to think about his child inhaling
the cotton dust and insecticide. When his eyes happened
on her and Mattie, their backs bent way over, he quickly
averted them. Once when he jerked his eyes away, he
found instead the bright-yellow school bus bouncing
along the road.

Frankie learned quickly how to chop the cotton, and
sometimes she even seemed to enjoy herself. Often the
choppers would go to the store to buy sardines and
crackers and beans for their dinner instead of going home.
At the store the Old Man would eat his beans from their
jagged-edge can and watch with pride as Frankie laughed
and talked with everyone and made dates with the ladies
to attend church on the different plantations. Every Sunday, Frankie had a service to go to. Sometimes, when his
head wasn't bad from drinking, the Old Man went with
her, because he liked so much to see her enjoy herself.
Those times, he put a few gallons of his whiskey in the

back of the car just in case somebody needed them. When he and Frankie went off to church like that, they didn't usually get back till late that night. They would be done sold all the whiskey and the Old Man would be talking loud about the wonderful sermon that the reverend had preached and all the souls that had come to Jesus.

That year, they finished the chopping in June. It was too late to send Frankie back to school, and she couldn't go again until after the cotton had been picked. When she went back, in November, she had missed four months and found it hard to keep up with the children who'd been going all the time. Still, she went every day that she could. She stayed home only when she had to, when her mother was sick, or when, in the cold weather, she didn't have shoes to wear.

Whenever she learned that she couldn't go to school on a particular day, she withdrew into herself for about an hour. She had a chair near the stove where she sat, and the little children knew not to bother her. After the hour, she'd push back her chair and go to stirring the cotton in the bed ticks or washing the greens for dinner.

If this was possible, the Old Man loved her still more now. He saw the children of the other workers and his own children, too, get discouraged and stop going to school. They said it was too confusing; they never knew what the teacher was talking about, because they'd not been there the day before or the month before. And they resented being left behind in classes with children half their size. He saw the other children get so that they wouldn't hold themselves up, wouldn't try to be clean and make folks respect them. Yet, every other day, Frankie managed to put on a clean, starched dress, and she kept at her lessons.

By the time Frankie was thirteen, she could figure as

well as the preacher, and she was made secretary of the church.

That same year, she asked her daddy if she could keep a record of what they made and what they spent.

"Sure, baby," he said. "I be proud for you to do it. We might even come out a little better this year when we settle up. I tell you what. If we get money outta Mr. White Junior this year, I'll buy you a dress for Christmas, a red one."

Frankie bought a black-and-white-speckled notebook. She put in it what they made and what they paid out on their bill. After chopping time, she became excited. She figured that they had just about paid the bill out. What they made from picking would be theirs. She and the Old Man would sit on the porch and go over the figures and plan for Christmas. Sometimes they even talked about taking a drive up to Chicago to see Uncle Ed. Every so often, he would try to hold down her excitement by reminding her that their figures had to be checked by the bossman's. Actually, he didn't expect to do much better than he'd done all the other years. But she was so proud to be using what she had learned, her numbers and all. He hated to discourage her.

Just before Christmas, they went to settle up. When it came to the Old Man's turn, he trembled a little. He knew it was almost too much to hope for, that they would have money coming to them. But some of Frankie's excitement had rubbed off on him.

He motioned to her, and they went up to the table, where there were several stacks of ten and twenty dollar bills, a big ledger, and a pistol. Mr. White Junior sat in the brown chair, and his agent stood behind him. Brown took heart from the absolute confidence with which Frankie Mae walked next to him, and he controlled his trembling. Maybe the child was right and they had something coming to them.

"Hey there, Johnnie," Mr. White Junior said, "see you brought Frankie Mae along. Fine, fine. Good to start them early. Here's you a seat."

The Old Man gave Frankie the one chair and stood beside her. The bossman rifled his papers and came out with a long, narrow sheet. Brown recognized his name at the top.

"Here you are, Johnnie, y'all come out pretty good this year. Proud of you. Don't owe but $65. Since you done so good, gonna let you have $100 for Christmas."

Frankie Mae spoke up. "I been keeping a book for my daddy. And I got some different figures. Let me show you."

The room was still. Everyone, while pretending not to notice the girl, was listening intently to what she said.

Mr. White Junior looked surprised, but he recovered quickly. "Why sure. Be glad to look at your figures. You know it's easy to make a mistake. I'll show you what you done wrong."

Brown clutched her shoulder to stop her from handing over the book. But it was too late. Already she was leaning over the table, comparing her figures with those in the ledger.

"See, Mr. White Junior, when we was chopping last year we made $576, and you took $320 of that to put on our bill. There. There it is on your book. And we borrowed $35 in July. There it is . . ."

The man behind the table grew red. One of his fat hands gripped the table while the other moved toward the pistol.

Frankie Mae finished. "So you see, you owe us $180 for the year."

The bossman stood up to gain the advantage of his

height. He seemed about to burst. His eyes flashed around
the room, and his hand clutched the pistol. He was just
raising it from the table when he caught hold of himself.
He took a deep breath and let go of the gun.

"Oh, yeah. I remember what happened now, Johnnie.
It was the slip I gave you to the doctor for Willie B. You
remember, last year, 'fore chopping time. I got the bill last
week. Ain't had time to put it in my book. It came to, let
me think. Yeah, that was the $350."

The Old Man's tension fell away from him, and he
resumed his normal manner. He knew exactly what the
bossman was saying. It was as he had expected, as it had
always been.

"Let's go, baby," he said.

But Frankie didn't get up from the chair. For a
moment, she looked puzzled. Then her face cleared. She
said, "Willie didn't have anything wrong with him
but a broken arm. The doctor spent twenty minutes with
him one time and ten the other. That couldn't a cost no
$350!"

The bossman's hand found the pistol again and gripped
it until the knuckles were white. Brown pulled Frankie to
him and put his arm around her. With his free hand he
fingered his own pistol, which he always carried in his
pocket. He was not afraid. But he hated the thought of
shooting the man; even if he just nicked him, it would be
the end for himself. He drew a line: If Mr. White Junior
touched him or Frankie, he would shoot. Short of that, he
would leave without a fight.

White spat thick, brown tobacco juice onto the floor,
spattering it on the Old Man and the girl. "Nigger," he
said, "I know you ain't disputing my word. Don't nobody
live on my place and call me a liar. That bill was $350.
You understand me?!" He stood tense, staring with hatred
at the man and the girl. Everyone waited for Brown to

answer. The Old Man felt Frankie's arms go 'round his waist.

"Tell him no, Daddy. We right, not him. I kept them figures all year, they got to be right." The gates of the state farm flashed through the Old Man's mind. He thought of Mattie, already sick from high blood, trying to make a living for eleven people. Frankie's arms tightened.

"Yessir," he said. "I understand."

The girl's arms dropped from him, and she started to the door. The other workers turned away to fiddle with a piece of rope to scold a child. Brown accepted the $50 that was thrown across the table to him. As he turned to follow Frankie, he heard Mr. White Junior's voice, low now and with a controlled violence. "Hey you, girl. You, Frankie Mae." She stopped at the door but didn't turn around.

"Long as you live, bitch, I'm gonna be right and you gonna be wrong. Now get your black ass outta here."

Frankie stumbled out to the car and crawled onto the back seat. She cried all the way home. Brown tried to quiet her. She could still have the red dress. They'd go down to the river tomorrow and start on a new batch of whiskey.

The next morning, he lay in bed waiting to hear Frankie Mae moving around and fussing, waiting to know that she had snapped back to her old self. He lay there until everyone in the house had gotten up. Still he did not hear her. Finally, he got up and went over to where she was balled up in the quilts.

He woke her. "Come on, baby. Time to get up. School bus be here soon."

"I ain't goin' today," she said; "got a stomach-ache."

Brown sat on the porch all day long, wishing that she would get up out the bed and struggling to understand what had happened. This time, Frankie had not bounced back to her old bright-eyed self. The line that held her to this self had been stretched too taut. It had lost its tension and couldn't pull her back.

Frankie never again kept a book for her daddy. She lost interest in things such as numbers and reading. She went to school as an escape from chores but got so little of her lessons done that she was never promoted from the fourth grade to the fifth. When she was fifteen, and in the fourth grade, she had her first child. After that, there was no more thought of school. In the following four years she had three more children.

She sat around the house, eating and growing fat. When well enough, she went to the field with her daddy. Her dresses were seldom ironed now. Whatever she could find to wear would do.

Still, there were a few times, maybe once every three or four months, when she was lively and fresh. She'd get dressed and clean the children up and have her daddy drive them to church. On such days she'd be the first one up. She would have food on the stove before anybody else had a chance to dress. Brown would load up his truck with his whiskey, and they'd stay all day.

It was for these isolated times that the Old Man waited. They kept him believing that she would get to be all right. Until she died, he woke up every morning listening for her laughter, waiting for her to pull the covers from his feet and scold him for being lazy.

She died giving birth to her fifth child. The midwife, Esther, was good enough, but she didn't know what to do when there were complications. Brown couldn't get up but sixty dollars of the hundred dollars cash that you had to deposit at the county hospital. So they wouldn't let Frankie in. She bled to death on the hundred-mile drive to the charity hospital in Vicksburg.

The Old Man squinted up at the fully risen sun. The

bossman was late. Should have been at the gate by now. Well, it didn't matter. Just a few more minutes and they'd be through with the place forever.

His thoughts went back to the time when the civil rights workers had first come around and they had started their meetings up at the store. They'd talked about voting and about how plantation workers should be making enough to live off of. Brown and the other men had listened and talked and agreed. So they decided to ask Mr. White Junior for a raise. They wanted nine dollars for their twelve-hour day.

They had asked. And he had said, Hell no. Before he'd raise them he'd lower them. So they agreed to ask him again. And if he still said no, they would go on strike.

At first, Brown hadn't understood himself why he agreed to the strike. It was only this morning that he realized why: It wasn't the wages or the house that was falling down 'round him and Mattie. It was that time when he went to ask Mr. White Junior about the other forty dollars that he needed to put Frankie in the hospital.

"Sorry, Johnnieboy," he'd said, patting Brown on the back, "but me and Miz White have a garden party today and I'm so busy. You know how women are. She want me there every minute. See me tomorrow. I'll fix you up then."

A cloud of dust rose up in front of Brown. The bossman was barreling down the road in his pickup truck. He was mad. That was what he did when he got mad, drove his truck up and down the road fast. Brown chuckled. When they got through with him this morning, he might run that truck into the river.

Mr. White Junior climbed down from the truck and made his way over to the gate. He began to give the orders for the day, who would drive the tractors, what fields would be chopped. The twelve men moved away from the fence, disdaining any support for what they were about to do.

One of the younger ones, James Lee, spoke up. "Mr. White Junior, we wants to know is you gonna raise us like we asked."

"No, goddammit. Now go on, do what I told you."

"Then," James Lee continued, "we got to go on strike from this place."

James Lee and the others left the gate and went to have a strategy meeting up at the store about what to do next.

The Old Man was a little behind the rest because he had something to give Mr. White Junior. He went over to the sweat-drenched, cursing figure and handed him the scarred timekeeper's watch, the watch that had ticked away Frankie Mae's youth in the hot, endless rows of cotton.

JEAN WHEELER SMITH

Jean Wheeler Smith was born in 1942 in Detroit. She received her B.S. in chemistry from Howard University, where she was elected to Phi Beta Kappa, and an M.S. in food science from the University of Maryland. While working for SNCC in 1964, she and her husband helped to set up a foundation through which several black families in the delta area of the Mississippi built their own concrete-block houses to replace tents and shacks. For a while, the Smiths operated a janitorial-supplies and household-goods store in Greenville, Mississippi, hoping to develop an economic basis for the black community. Ms. Smith now teaches full time at Federal City College in Washington, D.C., in the area of food science and nutrition. She has developed food co-operatives in Washington and is involved in research and experimentation with the problems of urban food production, a project aimed at helping people with very little land or resources develop control over their own food supply. She has published four short stories: "Frankie Mae" (in this anthology and in *Black Short Story Anthology*), "That She Would Dance No More" (in *Negro Digest*, January 1967); "The Machine" (in *Negro Digest*, November 1967); and "Somethin-to-Eat" (in *Black World*, June 1971); a play, *O.C.'s Heart* (in *Negro Digest*, April 1970); and many articles on science and nutrition.

In an essay entitled "I Learned to Feel Black," published in *The Black Power Revolt*, Jean Smith describes her experiences with SNCC (Student Nonviolent Coordinating Committee) organizing voters in Mississippi and with the Mississippi Freedom Democratic Party, challenging the all-white Mississippi Democratic Party. It is clear that Ms. Smith's experiences as a civil rights activist in the Deep South have forged an understanding of the black experience as it has been menaced by this society.

The four stories mentioned here are all set in the Deep South, mainly Mississippi, and they all deal with people who have been exploited and humiliated by segregation and by the spirit-and-body-crushing sharecropping system. Ossie Lee, in "That She Would Dance No More," is a black sharecropper, an old man at thirty-eight, whose life, like Frankie Mae's, has been a series of assaults on him. Carrying out the theme of the cyclic nature of oppression, Ossie Lee eventually takes out his frustrations on his young bride, assuring that she too will be beaten down by the life that has devastated him. But in almost all of her stories there is also the element of transcendence. As Frankie Mae's father finds the strength to oppose the system that has ticked away his daughter's life, many of her characters develop the resources to break through the cycle of oppression and despair. In Ms. Smith's own words, that cycle can be broken only by building a new black consciousness:

> For me and many other black people the only allowable conclusion from these experiences has been that Negroes must turn away from the preachings, assertions, and principles of the larger, white society and must turn inward to find the means whereby black people can lead full, meaningful lives. We must become conscious that our blackness calls for another set of principles on whose validity we can depend because they come from our own experiences.[*]

[*] "I Learned to Feel Black," in *The Black Power Revolt*, ed. by Floyd B. Barbour, Boston: Porter Sargent, 1968.

The Intimidation of Color

The Coming of Maureen Peal

TONI MORRISON

My daddy's face is a study. Winter moves into it and
presides there. His eyes become a cliff of snow threatening
to avalanche; his eyebrows bend like black limbs of leaf-
less trees. His skin takes on the pale, cheerless yellow of
winter sun; for a jaw he has the edges of a snowbound
field dotted with stubble; his high forehead is the frozen
sweep of the Erie, hiding currents of gelid thoughts that
eddy in darkness. Wolf killer turned hawk fighter, he
worked night and day to keep one from the door and
the other from under the windowsills. A Vulcan guarding
the flames, he gives us instructions about which doors
to keep closed or opened for proper distribution of heat,
lays kindling by, discusses qualities of coal, and teaches
us how to rake, feed, and bank the fire. And he will not
unrazor his lips until spring.

Winter tightened our heads with a band of cold and
melted our eyes. We put pepper in the feet of our stockings, Vaseline on our faces, and stared through dark ice-
box mornings at four stewed prunes, slippery lumps of
oatmeal, and cocoa with a roof of skin.

But mostly we waited for spring, when there could be
gardens.

By the time this winter had stiffened itself into a hateful knot that nothing could loosen, something did loosen
it, or rather someone. A someone who splintered the knot
into silver threads that tangled us, netted us, made us
long for the dull chafe of the previous boredom.

From *The Bluest Eye*.

This disrupter of seasons was a new girl in school named Maureen Peal. A high-yellow dream child with long brown hair braided into two lynch ropes that hung down her back. She was rich, at least by our standards, as rich as the richest of the white girls, swaddled in comfort and care. The quality of her clothes threatened to derange Frieda and me. Patent-leather shoes with buckles, a cheaper version of which we got only at Easter and which had disintegrated by the end of May. Fluffy sweaters the color of lemon drops tucked into skirts with pleats so orderly they astounded us. Brightly colored knee socks with white borders, a brown velvet coat trimmed in white rabbit fur, and a matching muff. There was a hint of spring in her sloe green eyes, something summery in her complexion, and a rich autumn ripeness in her walk.

She enchanted the entire school. When teachers called on her, they smiled encouragingly. Black boys didn't trip her in the halls; white boys didn't stone her, white girls didn't suck their teeth when she was assigned to be their work partners; black girls stepped aside when she wanted to use the sink in the girls' toilet, and their eyes genuflected under sliding lids. She never had to search for anybody to eat with in the cafeteria—they flocked to the table of her choice, where she opened fastidious lunches, shaming our jelly-stained bread with egg-salad sandwiches cut into four dainty squares, pink-frosted cupcakes, sticks of celery and carrots, proud, dark apples. She even bought and liked white milk.

Frieda and I were bemused, irritated, and fascinated by her. We looked hard for flaws to restore our equilibrium, but had to be content at first with uglying up her name, changing Maureen Peal to Meringue Pie. Later a minor epiphany was ours when we discovered that she had a dog tooth—a charming one to be sure—but a dog tooth nonetheless. And when we found out that she had been born with six fingers on each hand and that there was a little bump where each extra one had been removed, we smiled. They were small triumphs, but we took what we could get—snickering behind her back and calling her Six-finger-dog-tooth-meringue-pie. But we had to do it alone, for none of the other girls would co-operate with our hostility. They adored her.

When she was assigned a locker next to mine, I could indulge my jealousy four times a day. My sister and I both suspected that we were secretly prepared to be her friend, if she would let us, but I knew it would be a dangerous friendship, for when my eye traced the white border patterns of those Kelly-green knee socks, and felt the pull and slack of my brown stockings, I wanted to kick her. And when I thought of the unearned haughtiness in her eyes, I plotted accidental slammings of locker doors on her hand.

As locker friends, however, we got to know each other a little, and I was even able to hold a sensible conversation with her without visualizing her fall off a cliff, or giggling my way into what I thought was a clever insult.

One day, while I waited at the locker for Frieda, she joined me.

"Hi."

"Hi."

"Waiting for your sister?"

"Uh-huh."

"Which way do you go home?"

"Down Twenty-first Street to Broadway."

"Why don't you go down Twenty-second Street?"

"'Cause I live on Twenty-first Street."

"Oh. I can walk that way, I guess. Partly, anyway."

"Free country."

Frieda came toward us, her brown stockings straining

at the knees because she had tucked the toe under to hide a hole in the foot.

"Maureen's gonna walk part way with us."

Frieda and I exchanged glances, her eyes begging my restraint, mine promising nothing.

It was a false spring day, which, like Maureen, had pierced the shell of a deadening winter. There were puddles, mud, and an inviting warmth that deluded us. The kind of day on which we draped our coats over our heads, left our galoshes in school, and came down with croup the following day. We always responded to the slightest change in weather, the most minute shifts in time of day. Long before seeds were stirring, Frieda and I were scruffing and poking at the earth, swallowing air, drinking rain. . . .

As we emerged from the school with Maureen, we began to molt immediately. We put our head scarves in our coat pockets, and our coats on our heads. I was wondering how to maneuver Maureen's fur muff into a gutter when a commotion in the playground distracted us. A group of boys was circling and holding at bay a victim, Pecola Breedlove.

Bay Boy, Woodrow Cain, Buddy Wilson, Junie Bug—like a necklace of semiprecious stones they surrounded her. Heady with the smell of their own musk, thrilled by the easy power of a majority, they gaily harassed her.

"Black e mo. Black e mo. Yadaddsleepsnekked. Black e mo black e mo ya dadd sleeps nekked. Black e mo . . ."

They had extemporized a verse made up of two insults about matters over which the victim had no control; the color of her skin and speculations on the sleeping habits of an adult, wildly fitting in its incoherence. That they themselves were black, or that their own father had similarly relaxed habits was irrelevant. It was their contempt for their own blackness that gave the first insult its teeth.

They seemed to have taken all of their smoothly cultivated ignorance, their exquisitely learned self-hatred, their
elaborately designed hopelessness and sucked it all up into
a fiery cone of scorn that had burned for ages in the hol-
lows of their minds—cooled—and spilled over lips of outrage, consuming whatever was in its path. They danced
a macabre ballet around the victim, whom, for their own
sake, they were prepared to sacrifice to the flaming pit.

> Black e mo Black e mo Ya daddy sleeps nekked.
> Stch ta ta stch ta ta
> stach ta ta ta ta ta

Pecola edged around the circle crying. She had dropped
her notebook, and covered her eyes with her hands.

We watched, afraid they might notice us and turn their
energies our way. Then Frieda, with set lips and Mama's
eyes, snatched her coat from her head and threw it on
the ground. She ran toward them and brought her books
down on Woodrow Cain's head. The circle broke. Woodrow Cain grabbed his head.

"Hey, girl!"

"You cut that out, you hear?" I had never heard Frieda's
voice so loud and clear.

Maybe because Frieda was taller than he was, maybe
because he saw her eyes, maybe because he had lost interest in the game, or maybe because he had a crush on
Frieda, in any case Woodrow looked frightened just long
enough to give her more courage.

"Leave her 'lone, or I'm gone tell everybody what you
did!"

Woodrow did not answer; he just walled his eyes.

Bay Boy piped up, "Go on, gal. Ain't nobody bothering
you."

"You shut up, Bullet Head." I had found my tongue.

"Who you calling Bullet Head?"

"I'm calling you Bullet Head, Bullet Head."

Frieda took Pecola's hand. "Come on."

"You want a fat lip?" Bay Boy drew back his fist at me.

"Yeah. Gimme one of yours."

"You gone get one."

Maureen appeared at my elbow, and the boys seemed reluctant to continue under her springtime eyes so wide with interest. They buckled in confusion, not willing to beat up three girls under her watchful gaze. So they listened to a budding male instinct that told them to pretend we were unworthy of their attention.

"Come on, man."

"Yeah. Come on. We ain't got time to fool with them."

Grumbling a few disinterested epithets, they moved away.

I picked up Pecola's notebook and Frieda's coat, and the four of us left the playground.

"Old Bullet Head, he's always picking on girls."

Frieda agreed with me. "Miss Forrester said he was in-corrigival."

"Really?" I didn't know what that meant, but it had enough of a doom sound in it to be true of Bay Boy.

While Frieda and I clucked on about the near fight, Maureen, suddenly animated, put her velvet-sleeved arm through Pecola's and began to behave as though they were the closest of friends.

"I just moved here. My name is Maureen Peal. What's yours?"

"Pecola."

"Pecola? Wasn't that the name of the girl in *Imitation of Life*?"

"I don't know. What is that?"

"The picture show, you know. Where this mulatto girl hates her mother 'cause she is black and ugly but then cries at the funeral. It was real sad. Everybody cries in it. Claudette Colbert too."

"Oh." Pecola's voice was no more than a sigh.

"Anyway, her name was Pecola too. She was so pretty. When it comes back, I'm going to see it again. My mother has seen it four times."

Frieda and I walked behind them, surprised at Maureen's friendliness to Pecola, but pleased. Maybe she wasn't so bad, after all. Frieda had put her coat back on her head, and the two of us, so draped, trotted along enjoying the warm breeze and Frieda's heroics.

"You're in my gym class, aren't you?" Maureen asked Pecola.

"Yes."

"Miss Erkmeister's legs sure are bow. I bet she thinks they're cute. How come she gets to wear real shorts, and we have to wear those old bloomers? I want to die every time I put them on."

Pecola smiled but did not look at Maureen.

"Hey." Maureen stopped short. "There's an Isaley's. Want some ice cream? I have money."

She unzipped a hidden pocket in her muff and pulled out a multifolded dollar bill. I forgave her those knee socks.

"My uncle sued Isaley's," Maureen said to the three of us. "He sued the Isaley's in Akron. They said he was disorderly and that that was why they wouldn't serve him, but a friend of his, a policeman, came in and beared the witness, so the suit went through."

"What's a suit?"

"It's when you can beat them up if you want to and won't anybody do nothing. Our family does it all the time. We believe in suits."

At the entrance to Isaley's, Maureen turned to Frieda and me, asking, "You all going to buy some ice cream?"

We looked at each other. "No," Frieda said.

Maureen disappeared into the store with Pecola.

Frieda looked placidly down the street; I opened my mouth, but quickly closed it. It was extremely important that the world not know that I fully expected Maureen to buy us some ice cream, that for the past 120 seconds I had been selecting the flavor, that I had begun to like Maureen, and that neither of us had a penny.

We supposed Maureen was being nice to Pecola because of the boys, and were embarrassed to be caught—even by each other—thinking that she would treat us, or that we deserved it as much as Pecola did.

The girls came out. Pecola with two dips of orange-pineapple, Maureen with black raspberry.

"You should have got some," she said. "They had all kinds. Don't eat down to the tip of the cone," she advised Pecola.

"Why?"

"Because there's a fly in there."

"How you know?"

"Oh, not really. A girl told me she found one in the bottom of hers once, and ever since then she throws that part away."

"Oh."

We passed the Dreamland Theater, and Betty Grable smiled down at us.

"Don't you just love her?" Maureen asked.

"Uh-huh," said Pecola.

I differed. "Hedy Lamarr is better."

Maureen agreed. "Ooooo yes. My mother told me that a girl named Audrey, she went to the beauty parlor where we lived before, and asked the lady to fix her hair like Hedy Lamarr's, and the lady said, 'Yeah, when you grow some hair like Hedy Lamarr's.'" She laughed long and sweet.

"Sounds crazy," said Frieda.

"She sure is. Do you know she doesn't even menstrate yet, and she's sixteen. Do you, yet?"

"Yes." Pecola glanced at us.

"So do I." Maureen made no attempt to disguise her pride. "Two months ago I started. My girl friend in Toledo, where we lived before, said when she started she was scared to death. Thought she had killed herself."

"Do you know what it's for?" Pecola asked the question as though hoping to provide the answer herself.

"For babies." Maureen raised two pencil-stroke eyebrows at the obviousness of the question. "Babies need blood when they are inside you, and if you are having a baby, then you don't menstrate. But when you're not having a baby, then you don't have to save the blood, so it comes out."

"How do babies get the blood?" asked Pecola.

"Through the like-line. You know. Where your belly button is. That is where the like-line grows from and pumps the blood to the baby."

"Well, if the belly buttons are to grow like-lines to give the baby blood, and only girls have babies, how come boys have belly buttons?"

Maureen hesitated. "I don't know," she admitted. "But boys have all sorts of things they don't need." Her tinkling laughter was somehow stronger than our nervous ones. She curled her tongue around the edge of the cone, scooping up a dollop of purple that made my eyes water. We were waiting for a stop light to change. Maureen kept scooping the ice cream from around the cone's edge with her tongue; she didn't bite the edge as I would have done. Her tongue circled the cone. Pecola had finished hers; Maureen evidently liked her things to last. While I was thinking about her ice cream, she must have been thinking about her last remark, for she said to Pecola, "Did you ever see a naked man?"

Pecola blinked, then looked away. "No. Where would I see a naked man?"

"I don't know. I just asked."

"I wouldn't even look at him, even if I did see him. That's dirty. Who wants to see a naked man?" Pecola was agitated. "Nobody's father would be naked in front of his own daughter. Not unless he was dirty too."

"I didn't say 'father.' I just said 'a naked man.'"

"Well . . ."

"How come you said 'father'?" Maureen wanted to know.

"Who else would she see, dog tooth?" I was glad to have a chance to show anger. Not only because of the ice cream, but because we had seen our own father naked and didn't care to be reminded of it and feel the shame brought on by the absence of shame. He had been walking down the hall from the bathroom into his bedroom and passed the open door of our room. We had lain there wide-eyed. He stopped and looked in, trying to see in the dark room whether we were really asleep—or was it his imagination that opened eyes were looking at him? Apparently he convinced himself that we were sleeping. He moved away, confident that his little girls would not lie open-eyed like that, staring, staring. When he had moved on, the dark took only him away, not his nakedness. That stayed in the room with us. Friendly-like.

"I'm not talking to you," said Maureen. "Besides, I don't care if she sees her father naked. She can look at him all day if she wants to. Who cares?"

"You do," said Frieda. "That's all you talk about."

"It is not."

"It is so. Boys, babies, and somebody's naked daddy. You must be boy-crazy."

"You better be quiet."

"Who's gonna make me?" Frieda put her hand on her hip and jutted her face toward Maureen.

"You all ready made. Mammy made."

"You stop talking about my mama."

"Well, you stop talking about my daddy."

"Who said anything about your old daddy?"

"You did."

"Well, you started it."

"I wasn't even talking to you. I was talking to Pecola."

"Yeah. About seeing her naked daddy."

"So what if she did see him?"

Pecola shouted, "I never saw my daddy naked. Never."

"You did too," Maureen snapped. "Bay Boy said so."

"I did not."

"You did."

"I did not."

"Did. Your own daddy, too!"

Pecola tucked her head in—a funny, sad, helpless movement. A kind of hunching of the shoulders, pulling in of the neck, as though she wanted to cover her ears.

"You stop talking about her daddy," I said.

"What do I care about her old black daddy?" asked Maureen.

"Black? Who you calling black?"

"You!"

"You think you so cute!" I swung at her and missed, hitting Pecola in the face. Furious at my clumsiness, I threw my notebook at her, but it caught her in the small of her velvet back, for she had turned and was flying across the street against traffic.

Safe on the other side, she screamed at us, "I *am* cute! And you ugly! Black and ugly black e mos. I *am* cute!"

She ran down the street, the green knee socks making her legs look like wild dandelion stems that had somehow lost their heads. The weight of her remark stunned us, and it was a second or two before Frieda and I collected ourselves enough to shout, "Six-finger-dog-tooth-meringue-pie!" We chanted this most powerful of our arsenal of insults as long as we could see the green stems and rabbit fur.

Grown people frowned at the three girls on the curb-side, two with their coats draped over their heads, the collars framing the eyebrows like nuns' habits, black garters showing where they bit the tops of brown stock-ings that barely covered the knees, angry faces knotted like dark cauliflowers.

Pecola stood a little apart from us, her eyes hinged in the direction in which Maureen had fled. She seemed to fold into herself, like a pleated wing. Her pain antag-onized me. I wanted to open her up, crisp her edges, ram a stick down that hunched and curving spine, force her to stand erect and spit the misery out on the streets. But she held it in where it could lap up into her eyes.

Frieda snatched her coat from her head. "Come on, Claudia. 'Bye, Pecola."

We walked quickly at first, and then slower, pausing every now and then to fasten garters, tie shoelaces, scratch, or examine old scars. We were sinking under the wisdom, accuracy, and relevance of Maureen's last words. If she was cute—and if anything could be believed, she *was*—then we were not. And what did that mean? We were lesser. Nicer, brighter, but still lesser. Dolls we could destroy, but we could not destroy the honey voices of parents and aunts, the obedience in the eyes of our peers, the slippery light in the eyes of our teachers when they encountered the Maureen Peals of the world. What was the secret? What did we lack? Why was it important? And so what? Guileless and without vanity, we were still in love with ourselves then. We felt comfortable in our skins, enjoyed the news that our senses released to us, admired our dirt, cultivated our scars, and could not comprehend this unworthiness. Jealousy we understood and thought natural—a desire to have what somebody else had; but envy was a strange, new feeling for us. And all the time we knew that Maureen Peal was not the Enemy and not worthy of such intense hatred. The *Thing* to fear was the *Thing* that made *her* beautiful, and not us.

TONI MORRISON

Born in Lorain, Ohio, on February 18, 1931, Toni Morrison received her B.A. from Howard University and an M.A. from Cornell. She was an instructor of English at Texas Southern University from 1955 to 1957 and at Howard from 1957 until 1964.

The author of two books, *The Bluest Eye* (1971) and *Sula* (1974), she is presently a senior editor at Random House.

In a review in *Freedomways* magazine (First Quarter 1974) Barbara Smith points out two identifying characteristics of Morrison's work: "As significant as her rootedness in Black life is the fact that her perspective is undeniably feminine." Both novels are written from the point of view of a black female, the little girl Claudia in *The Bluest Eye* and the two black women Nel and Sula in *Sula.* Both are also works that "rediscover black history" as they re-create the lives of black people in a small Ohio town. Morrison remembers the words, the sights, the sounds, and the rituals of the black past. In a word or phrase, she is able to capture the humor as well as the terror of that experience; she makes us understand how some survived whole and why others were destroyed. Morrison's emphasis on the importance of black past as it was really lived, not as it was imagined, led her to help three collectors of black memorabilia to produce *The Black Book*, an informal, unconventional history of black people.

Although Morrison celebrates black life in her perfect re-creation of it, she does not miss the essential tragic loss that occurs in the lives of black women. The four major characters in her two novels—Claudia, Pecola, Nel, and Sula—all suffer the peculiar tragedies that racial and sexual circumstances have forced upon them. Somewhere, buried deep inside of Sula, for example, is the soul and energy of an artist, but because she is a black woman growing up in 1927, she does not have paints or clay or the dance to use up her tremendous undisciplined restlessness, and her restlessness finally makes her dangerous. Her friend, Nel, on the other hand, chooses marriage, a choice that Morrison describes in chilling terms: In marrying Jude, Nel will become like the hem of Jude's garment, "the tuck and fold that hid his raveling edges . . . the two of them together would make one Jude." Nel will be consumed in the process of making an improved version of Jude.

At the end of that novel, Sula dies of cancer at the age of thirty; Nel is alone with the pain and grief of being left by both her husband and her best friend. At the end of *The Bluest Eye*, Pecola, having been raped by her father, goes mad; and Claudia and Frieda have been initiated into the terror of loving white dolls and Shirley Temple.

If You're Light and Have Long Hair

GWENDOLYN BROOKS

Came the invitation that Paul recognized as an honor of the first water, and as sufficient indication that he was, at last, a social somebody. The invitation was from the Foxy Cats Club, the club of clubs. He was to be present, in formal dress, at the Annual Foxy Cats Dawn Ball. No chances were taken: "Top hat, white tie and tails" hastily followed the "Formal dress," and that elucidation was in bold type.

Twenty men were in the Foxy Cats Club. All were good-looking. All wore clothes that were rich and suave. All "handled money," for their number consisted of well-located barbers, policemen, "government men," and men with a lucky touch at the tracks. Certainly the Foxy Cats Club was not a representative of that growing group of South Side organizations devoted to moral and civic improvements, or to literary or other cultural pursuits. If that had been so, Paul would have chucked his bid (which was black and silver, decorated with winking cat faces) down the toilet with a yawn. "That kind of stuff" was hardly understood by Paul, and was always dismissed with an airy "dicty," "hincty," or "highfalutin." But no. The Foxy Cats devoted themselves solely to the business of being "hep," and each year they spent hundreds of dollars on their wonderful Dawn Ball, which did not

From the novel *Maud Martha*.

begin at dawn, but was scheduled to end at dawn. "Ball," they called the frolic, but it served also the purposes of party, feast, and fashion show. Maud Martha, watching him study his invitation, watching him lift his chin, could see that he considered himself one of the blessed.

Who—what kind soul had recommended him!

"He'll have to take me," thought Maud Martha. "For the envelope is addressed 'Mr. and Mrs.,' and I opened it. I guess he'd like to leave me home. At the Ball, there will be only beautiful girls, or real stylish ones. There won't be more than a handful like me. My type is not a Foxy Cat favorite. But he can't avoid taking me—since he hasn't yet thought of words or ways strong enough, and at the same time soft enough—for he's kind: he doesn't like to injure— to carry across to me the news that he is not to be held permanently by my type, and that he can go on with this marriage only if I put no ropes or questions around him. Also, he'll want to humor me, now that I'm pregnant."

She would need a good dress. That, she knew, could be a problem, on his grocery clerk's pay. He would have his own expenses. He would have to rent his topper and tails, and he would have to buy a fine tie, and really excellent shoes. She knew he was thinking that on the strength of his appearance and sophisticated behavior at this Ball might depend his future admission (for why not dream?) to *membership*, actually, in the Foxy Cats Club!

"I'll settle," decided Maud Martha, "on a plain white princess-style thing and some blue and black satin ribbon. I'll go to my mother's. I'll work miracles at the sewing machine.

"On that night, I'll wave my hair. I'll smell faintly of lily of the valley."

The main room of the Club 99, where the Ball was held, was hung with green and yellow and red balloons, and the thick pillars, painted to give an effect of marble, and stretching from floor to ceiling, were draped with green and red and yellow crepe paper. Huge ferns, rubber plants, and bowls of flowers were at every corner. The floor itself was a decoration, golden, glazed. There was no overhead light; only wall lamps, and the bulbs in these were romantically dim. At the back of the room, standing on a furry white rug, was the long banquet table, dressed in damask, accented by groups of thin silver candlesticks bearing white candles, and laden with lovely food: cold chicken, lobster, candied ham fruit combinations, potato salad in a great gold dish, corn sticks, a cheese fluff in spiked tomato cups, fruit cake, angel cake, sunshine cake. The drinks were at a smaller table nearby, behind which stood a genial mixologist, quick with maraschino cherries, and with lemon, ice, and liquor. Wines were there, and whiskey, and rum, and eggnog made with pure cream.

Paul and Maud Martha arrived rather late, on purpose. Rid of their wraps, they approached the glittering floor. Bunny Bates's orchestra was playing Ellington's "Solitude."

Paul, royal in rented finery, was flushed with excitement. Maud Martha looked at him. Not very tall. Not very handsomely made. But there was that extraordinary quality of maleness. Hiding in the body that was not *too* yellow, waiting to spring out at her, surround her (she liked to think)—that maleness. The Ball stirred her. The Beauties, in their gorgeous gowns, bustling, supercilious; the young men, who at other times most unpleasantly blew their noses, and darted surreptitiously into alleys to relieve themselves, and sweated and swore at their jobs, and scratched their more intimate parts, now smiling, smooth, overgallant; the drowsy lights; the smells of food and flowers, the smell of Murray's pomade, the body perfumes, natural and superimposed; the sensuous heaviness

of the wine-colored draperies at the many windows; the
music, now steamy and slow, now as clear and fragile as
glass, now raging, passionate, now moaning and thickly
gray. The Ball made toys of her emotions, stirred her
variously. But she was anxious to have it end, she was anxious to be at home again, with the door closed behind herself and her husband. Then, he might be warm. There
might be more than the absent courtesy he had been giving her of late. Then, he might be the tree she had a great
need to lean against, in this "emergency." There was no
telling what dear thing he might say to her, what little
gem let fall.

But, to tell the truth, his behavior now was not very
promising of gems to come. After their second dance he
escorted her to a bench by the wall, left her. Trying to
look nonchalant, she sat. She sat, trying not to show the
inferiority she did not feel. When the music struck up
again, he began to dance with someone red-haired and
curved, and white as a white. Who was she? He had
approached her easily, he had taken her confidently, he
held her and conversed with her as though he had known
her well for a long, long time. The girl smiled up at
him. Her gold-spangled bosom was pressed—was pressed
against that maleness—

A man asked Maud Martha to dance. He was dark, too.
His mustache was small.

"Is this your first Foxy Cats?" he asked.

"What?" Paul's cheek was on that of Gold-Spangles.

"First Cats?"

"Oh. Yes." Paul and Gold-Spangles were weaving
through the noisy twisting couples, were trying, apparently, to get to the reception hall.

"Do you know that girl? What's her name?" Maud
Martha asked her partner, pointing to Gold-Spangles. Her
partner looked, nodded. He pressed her closer.

"That's Maella. That's Maella."

"Pretty, isn't she?" She wanted him to keep talking about Maella. He nodded again.

"Yep. She has 'em howling along the stroll, all right, all right."

Another man, dancing past with an artificial redhead, threw a whispered word at Maud Martha's partner, who caught it eagerly, winked. "Solid, ol' man," he said. "Solid, Jack." He pressed Maud Martha closer. "You're a babe," he said. "You're a real babe." He reeked excitingly of tobacco, liquor, pinesoap, toilet water, and Sen Sen.

Maud Martha thought of her parents' back yard. Fresh. Clean. Smokeless. In her childhood, a snowball bush had shone there, big above the dandelions. The snowballs had been big, healthy. Once, she and her sister and brother had waited in the back yard for their parents to finish readying themselves for a trip to Milwaukee. The snowballs had been so beautiful, so fat and startlingly white in the sunlight, that she had suddenly loved home a thousand times more than ever before, and had not wanted to go to Milwaukee. But as the children grew, the bush sickened. Each year, the snowballs were smaller and more dispirited. Finally a summer came when there were no blossoms at all. Maud Martha wondered what had become of the bush. For it was not there now. Yet she, at least, had never seen it go.

"Not," thought Maud Martha, "that they love each other. It oughta be that simple. Then I could lick it. It oughta be that easy. But it's my color that makes him mad. I try to shut my eyes to that, but it's no good. What I am inside, what is really me, he likes okay. But he keeps looking at my color, which is like a wall. He has to jump over it in order to meet and touch what I've got for him. He has to jump away up high in order to see it. He gets awful tired of all that jumping."

Paul came back from the reception hall. Maella was clinging to his arm. A final cry of the saxophone finished that particular slice of the blues. Maud Martha's partner bowed, escorted her to a chair by a rubber plant, bowed again, left.

"I could," considered Maud Martha, "go over there and scratch her upsweep down. I could spit on her back. I could scream. 'Listen,' I could scream, 'I'm making a baby for this man and I mean to do it in peace.'"

But if the root was sour what business did she have up there hacking at a leaf?

The Black Woman and the
Myth of the White Woman

The Self-Solace

GWENDOLYN BROOKS

Sonia Johnson got together her towels and soap. She scrubbed out her bowls. She mixed her water.

Maud Martha, waiting, was quiet. It was pleasant to let her mind go blank. And here in the beauty shop that was not a difficult thing to do. For the perfumes in the great jars, to be sold for twelve dollars and fifty cents an ounce and one dollar a dram, or seven dollars and fifty cents an ounce and one dollar a dram, the calendars, the bright signs extolling the virtues of Lily cologne (Made by the Management), the limp lengths of detached human hair, the pile of back-number *Vogues* and *Bazaars,* the earrings and clasps and beaded bags, white blouses—the "side line" —these things did not force themselves into the mind and make a disturbance there. One was and was not aware of them. Could sit here and think, or not think, of problems. Think, or not. One did not have to, if one wished not.

"If she burns me today—if she yanks at my hair—if she calls me sweetheart or dahlin'—"

Sonia Johnson parted the hangings that divided her reception room from her workrooms. "Come on back, baby doll."

But just then the bell tinkled, and in pushed a young white woman, wearing a Persian lamb coat, and a Persian lamb cap with black satin ribbon swirled capably in a soft knot at the back.

"Yes," thought Maud Martha, "it's legitimate. It's

From the novel *Maud Martha.*

November. It's not cold, but it's cool. You can wear your new fur now and not be laughed at by too many people."

The young white woman introduced herself to Mrs. Johnson as Miss Ingram, and said that she had new toilet waters, a make-up base that was so good it was "practically impossible," and a new lipstick.

"No make-up bases," said Sonia. "And no toilet water. We create our own."

"This new lipstick, this new shade," Miss Ingram said, taking it out of a smart little black bag, "is just the thing for your customers. For their dark complexions."

Sonia Johnson looked interested. She always put herself out to be kind and polite to these white salesmen and saleswomen. Some beauticians were brusque. They were almost insulting. They were glad to have the whites at their mercy, if only for a few moments. They made them crawl. Then they applied the whiplash. Then they sent the poor creatures off—with no orders. Then they laughed and laughed and laughed, a terrible laughter. But Sonia Johnson was not that way. She liked to be kind and polite. She liked to be merciful. She did not like to take advantage of her power. Indeed, she felt it was better to strain, to bend far back, to spice one's listening with the smooth smile, the quick and attentive nod, the well-timed "sure" or "uh-huh." She was against this eye-for-eye-tooth-for-tooth stuff.

Maud Martha looked at Miss Ingram's beautiful legs, wondered where she got the sheer stockings that looked like bare flesh at the same time that they did not, wondered if Miss Ingram knew that in the "Negro group" there were complexions whiter than her own, and other complexions, brown, tan, yellow, cream, which could not take a dark lipstick and keep their poise. Maud Martha picked up an ancient *Vogue*, turned the pages.

"What's the lipstick's name?" Sonia Johnson asked.

"Black Beauty," Miss Ingram said, with firm-lipped determination. "You won't regret adding it to your side line, I assure you, madam."

"What's it sell for?"

"A dollar and a half. Let me leave you—say, ten—and in a week I'll come back and find them all gone, and you'll be here clamoring for more, I know you will. I'll leave ten."

"Well. Okay."

"That's fine, madam. Now, I'll write down your name and address—"

Sonia rattled them off for her. Miss Ingram wrote them down. Then she closed her case.

"Now, I'll take just five dollars. Isn't that reasonable? You don't pay the rest till they're all sold. Oh, I know you're going to be just terribly pleased. And your customers too, Mrs. Johnson."

Sonia opened her cash drawer and took out five dollars for Miss Ingram. Miss Ingram brightened. The deal was closed. She pushed back a puff of straw-colored hair that had slipped from under her Persian lamb cap and fallen over the faint rose of her cheek.

"I'm mighty glad," she confided, "that the cold weather is in. I love the cold. It was awful, walking the streets in that nasty old August weather. And even September was rather close this year, didn't you think?"

Sonia agreed. "Sure was."

"People," confided Miss Ingram, "think this is a snap job. It ain't. I work like a nigger to make a few pennies. A few lousy pennies."

Maud Martha's head shot up. She did not look at Miss Ingram. She stared intently at Sonia Johnson. Sonia Johnson's sympathetic smile remained. Her eyes turned, as if magnetized, toward Maud Martha; but she forced her smile to stay on. Maud Martha went back to *Vogue*.

"For," she thought, "I must have been mistaken. I was afraid I heard that woman say 'nigger.' Apparently not. Because of course Mrs. Johnson wouldn't let her get away with it. In her own shop." Maud Martha closed *Vogue*. She began to consider what she herself might have said, had she been Sonia Johnson, and had the woman really said "nigger." "I wouldn't curse. I wouldn't holler. I'll bet Mrs. Johnson would do both those things. And I could understand her wanting to, all right. I would be gentle in a cold way. I would give her, not a return insult—directly, at any rate!—but information. I would get it across to her that—" Maud Martha stretched. "But I wouldn't insult her." Maud Martha began to take the hairpins out of her hair. "I'm glad, though, that she didn't say it. She's pretty and pleasant. If she had said it, I would feel all strained and tied up inside, and I would feel that it was my duty to help Mrs. Johnson get it settled, to help clear it up in some way. I'm too relaxed to fight today. Sometimes fighting is interesting. Today, it would have been just plain old ugly duty."

"Well, I wish you success with Black Beauty," Miss Ingram said, smiling in a tired manner, as she buttoned the top button of her Persian lamb. She walked quickly out the door. The little bell tinkled charmingly.

Sonia Johnson looked at her customer with thoughtful, narrowed eyes. She walked over, dragged a chair up close. She sat. She began to speak in a dull, level tone.

"You know, why I didn't catch her up on that, is—our people is got to stop feeling so sensitive about these words like 'nigger' and such. I often think about this, and how these words like 'nigger' don't mean to some of these here white people what our people *think* they mean. Now, 'nigger,' for instance, means to them something bad, or slavey-like, or low. They don't mean anything against me. I'm a Negro, not a 'nigger.' Now, a white man can be a 'nigger,' according to their meaning for the word, just like a colored man can. So why should I go getting all stepped up about a thing like that? Our people is got to stop getting all stepped up about every little thing, especially when it don't amount to nothing. . . ."

"You mean to say," Maud Martha broke in, "that that woman really did say 'nigger'?"

"Oh, yes, she said it, all right, but like I'm telling—"

"Well! At first, I thought she said it, but then I decided I must have been mistaken, because you weren't getting after her."

"Now that's what I'm trying to explain to you, dearie. Sure, I could have got all hot and bothered, and told her to clear out of here, or cussed her daddy, or something like that. But what would be the point, when, like I say, that word 'nigger' can mean one of them just as fast as one of us, and in fact it don't mean us, and in fact we're just too sensitive and all? What would be the point? Why make enemies? Why go getting all hot and bothered all the time?"

Maud Martha stared steadily into Sonia Johnson's irises. She said nothing. She kept on staring into Sonia Johnson's irises.

GWENDOLYN BROOKS

Born June 7, 1917, in Topeka, Kansas, Gwendolyn Brooks was reared in Chicago and has lived and worked there, on the South Side, for many years. Since 1945, when her first book of poetry, *A Street in Bronzeville*, appeared, Ms. Brooks has published nine books of poetry, one novel (*Maud Martha*, 1953), and an autobiography (*Report from Part One*, 1972). She is the editor of a periodical, *The Black Position*. She received a Pulitzer prize for her poetry in 1950 and is the poet laureate of Illinois.

Her work has always been characterized by an endur-
ing concern for the black urban poor, but that concern has
been manifest in her attention to the ordinary aspects of
ordinary black lives: "Her areas of concern are the small,
almost imperceptible psychological and economic webs
that trap common Black people in their urban enclaves."*

More specifically, Gwendolyn Brooks has shown a
special concern for the lives of black women, particularly
in her book of poetry *Annie Allen,* the theme of which is
the growth and development of a young black woman,
and in *Maud Martha,* a novel that traces the life of a dark-
skinned girl from her girlhood to the time she has her first
child. This novel and many of her poems also show Ms.
Brooks's sensitivity to the unique problems of the dark-
skinned black woman.

In her thirty-year writing career, Ms. Brooks has shown
continual growth. She remarks in her autobiography that
had she died before she was fifty, she would have died a
" 'Negro' fraction." One of the major changes in her life
and in her work since the age of fifty has been an open
and conscious adoption of a more militant stance as a
writer, as evidenced by her rejection of her earlier, "in-
tegrationist" poetry. She considers her change to a black
publishing company—Broadside Press—another major
change in her life.

* *Black Writers of America,* ed. Richard Barksdale and Keneth
Kinnamon (New York: The Macmillan Company, 1972), p.
714.

A Happening in Barbados

LOUISE M. MERIWETHER

The best way to pick up a Barbadian man, I hoped, was to walk alone down the beach with my tall, brown frame squeezed into a skintight bathing suit. Since my hotel was near the beach, and Dorothy and Alison, my two traveling companions, had gone shopping, I managed this quite well. I had not taken more than a few steps on the glittering, white sand before two black men were on either side of me vying for attention.

I chose the tall, slim-hipped one over the squat, muscle-bound man who was also grinning at me. But apparently they were friends, because Edwin had no sooner settled me under his umbrella than the squat one showed up with a beach chair and two other boys in tow.

Edwin made the introductions. His temporary rival was Gregory, and the other two were Alphonse and Dimitri.

Gregory was ugly. He had thick, rubbery lips, a scarcity of teeth, and a broad nose splattered like a pyramid across his face. He was all massive shoulders and bulging biceps. No doubt he had a certain animal magnetism, but personally I preferred a lean man like Edwin, who was well built but slender, his whole body fitting together like a symphony. Alphonse and Dimitri were clean-cut and pleasant looking.

They were all too young—twenty to twenty-five at the most—and Gregory seemed the oldest. I inwardly mourned their youth and settled down to make the most of my catch.

The crystal-blue sky rivaled the royal blue of the Carib-

bean for beauty, and our black bodies on the white sand
added to the munificence of colors. We ran into the sea
like squealing children when the sudden raindrops came,
then shivered on the sand under a makeshift tent of
umbrellas and damp towels waiting for the sun to reap-
pear while nourishing ourselves with straight Barbados
rum.

As with most of the West Indians I had already met on
my whirlwind tour of Trinidad and Jamaica, who wel-
comed American Negroes with open arms, my new
friends loved their island home, but work was scarce and
they yearned to go to America. They were hungry for
news of how Negroes were faring in the States.

Edwin's arm rested casually on my knee in a proprie-
tary manner, and I smiled at him. His thin, serious face
was smooth, too young for a razor, and when he smiled
back, he looked even younger. He told me he was a waiter
at the Hilton, saving his money to make it to the States. I
had already learned not to be snobbish with the island's
help. Yesterday's waiter may be tomorrow's prime
minister.

Dimitri, very black with an infectious grin, was also a
waiter, and lanky Alphonse was a tile setter.

Gregory's occupation was apparently women, for that's
all he talked about. He was able to launch this subject
when a bony white woman—more peeling red than white,
really looking like a gaunt cadaver in a loose-fitting bathing suit—came out of the sea and walked up to us. She
smiled archly at Gregory.

"Are you going to take me to the Pigeon Club tonight,
sugar?"

"No, mon," he said pleasantly, with a toothless grin.
"I'm taking a younger pigeon."

The woman turned a deeper red, if that was possible,
and, mumbling something incoherent, walked away.

"That one is always after me to take her some place," Gregory said. "She's rich, and she pays the bills but, mon, I don't want an old hag nobody else wants. I like to take my women away from white men and watch them squirm."

"Come down, mon," Dimitri said, grinning. "She look like she's starving for what you got to spare."

We all laughed. The boys exchanged stories about their experiences with predatory white women who came to the islands looking for some black action. But, one and all, they declared they liked dark-skinned meat the best, and I felt like a black queen of the Nile when Gregory winked at me and said, "The blacker the berry, mon, the sweeter the juice."

They had all been pursued and had chased some white tail, too, no doubt, but while the others took it all in good humor, it soon became apparent that Gregory's exploits were exercises in vengeance.

Gregory was saying: "I told that bastard, 'You in my country now, mon, and I'll kick your ass all the way back to Texas. The girl agreed to dance with me, and she don't need your permission.' That white man's face turned purple, but he sat back down, and I dance with his girl. Mon, they hate to see me rubbing bellies with their women because they know once she rub bellies with me she wanna rub something else, too." He laughed, and we all joined in. Serves the white men right, I thought. Let's see how they liked licking *that* end of the stick for a change.

"Mon, you gonna get killed yet," Edwin said, moving closer to me on the towel we shared. "You're crazy. You don't care whose woman you mess with. But it's not gonna be a white man who kill you but some bad Bajan."

Gregory led in the laughter, then held us spellbound for the next hour with intimate details of his affair with Glenda, a young white girl spending the summer with her father on their yacht. Whatever he had, Glenda wanted it desperately, or so Gregory told it.

Yeah, I thought to myself, like LSD, a black lover is the thing this year. I had seen the white girls in the Village and at off-Broadway theaters clutching their black men tightly while I, manless, looked on with bitterness. I often vowed I would find me an ofay in self-defense, but I could never bring myself to condone the wholesale rape of my slave ancestors by letting a white man touch me.

We finished the rum, and the three boys stood up to leave, making arrangements to get together later with us and my two girl friends and go clubbing.

Edwin and I were left alone. He stretched out his muscled leg and touched my toes with his. I smiled at him and let our thighs come together. Why did he have to be so damned young? Then our lips met, his warm and demanding, and I thought, what the hell, maybe I will. I was thirty-nine—good-bye, sweet bird of youth—an ungay divorcee, uptight and drinking too much, trying to disown the years which had brought only loneliness and pain. I had clawed my way up from the slums of Harlem via night school and was now a law clerk on Wall Street. But the fight upward had taken its toll. My husband, who couldn't claw as well as I, got lost somewhere in that concrete jungle. The last I saw of him, he was peering under every skirt around, searching for his lost manhood.

I had always felt contempt for women who found their kicks by robbing the cradle. Now here I was on a Barbados beach with an amorous child young enough to be my son. Two sayings flitted unbidden across my mind. "Judge not, that ye be not judged" and "The thing which I feared is come upon me." I thought, ain't it the goddamned truth?

Edwin kissed me again, pressing the length of his body against mine.

"I've got to go," I gasped. "My friends have probably returned and are looking for me. About ten tonight?"

He nodded; I smiled at him and ran all the way to my hotel.

At exactly ten o'clock, the telephone in our room announced we had company downstairs.

"Hot damn," Alison said, putting on her eyebrows in front of the mirror. "We're not going to be stood up."

"Island men," I said loftily, "are dependable, not like the bums you're used to in America."

Alison, freckled and willowy, had been married three times and was looking for her fourth. Her motto was, if at first you don't succeed, find another mother. She was a real-estate broker in Los Angeles, and we had been childhood friends in Harlem.

"What I can't stand," Dorothy said from the bathroom, "are those creeps who come to your apartment, drink up your liquor, then dirty up your sheets. You don't even get a dinner out of the deal."

She came out of the bathroom in her slip. Petite and delicate with a pixie grin, at thirty-five Dorothy looked more like one of the high school girls she taught than their teacher. She had never been married. Years before, while she was holding onto her virginity with a miser's grip, her fiancé messed up and knocked up one of her friends.

Since then, all of Dorothy's affairs had been with married men, displaying perhaps a subconscious vendetta against all wives.

By ten-twenty we were downstairs and I was introducing the girls to our four escorts, who eyed us with unconcealed admiration. We were looking good in our Saks Fifth Avenue finery. They were looking good, too, in soft shirts and loose slacks, all except Gregory, whose bulging

muscles confined in clothing made him seem more gargan-
tuan.

We took a cab and a few minutes later were squeezing
behind a table in a small, smoky room called the Pigeon
Club. A Trinidad steel band was blasting out the walls,
and the tiny dance area was jammed with wiggling bot-
toms and shuffling feet. The white tourists trying to do
the hip-shaking calypso were having a ball and looking
awkward.

I got up to dance with Edwin. He had a natural grace
and was easy to follow. Our bodies found the rhythm and
became one with it while our eyes locked in silent ancient
combat, his pleading, mine teasing.

We returned to our seats and to tall glasses of rum and
cola tonic. The party had begun.

I danced every dance with Edwin, his clasp becoming
gradually tighter until my face was smothered in his
shoulder, my arms locked around his neck. He was ador-
able. Very good for my ego. The other boys took turns
dancing with my friends, but soon preferences were set—
Alison with Alphonse and Dorothy with Dimitri. With
good humor, Gregory ordered another round and didn't
seem to mind being odd man out, but he wasn't alone for
long.

During the floor show, featuring the inevitable limbo
dancers, a pretty white girl, about twenty-two, with
straight, red hair hanging down to her shoulder, appeared
at Gregory's elbow. From his wink at me and self-satisfied
grin, I knew this was Glenda from the yacht.

"Hello," she said to Gregory. "Can I join you, or do you
have a date?"

Well, I thought, that's the direct approach.

"What are you doing here?" Gregory asked.

"Looking for you."

Gregory slid over on the bench, next to the wall, and

Glenda sat down as he introduced her to the rest of us. Somehow, her presence spoiled my mood. We had been happy being black, and I resented this intrusion from the white world. But Glenda was happy. She had found the man she'd set out to find and a swinging party to boot. She beamed a dazzling smile around the table.

Alphonse led Alison onto the dance floor, and Edwin and I followed. The steel band was playing a wild calypso, and I could feel my hair rising with the heat as I joined in the wildness.

When we returned to the table, Glenda applauded us, then turned to Gregory. "Why don't you teach me to dance like that?"

He answered with his toothless grin and a leer, implying he had better things to teach her.

White women were always snatching our men, I thought, and now they want to dance like us.

I turned my attention back to Edwin and met his full stare.

I teased him with a smile, refusing to commit myself. He had a lusty, healthy appetite, which was natural, I supposed, for a twenty-one-year-old lad. Lord, but why did he have to be that young? I stood up to go to the ladies' room.

"Wait for me," Glenda cried, trailing behind me.

The single toilet stall was occupied, and Glenda leaned against the wall waiting for it while I flipped open my compact and powdered my grimy face.

"You married?" she asked.

"Divorced."

"When I get married, I want to stay hooked forever."

"That's the way I planned it, too," I said dryly.

"What I mean," she rushed on, "is that I've gotta find a cat who wants to groove only with me."

Oh Lord, I thought, don't try to sound like us, too. Use your own, sterile language.

"I really dug this guy I was engaged to," Glenda continued, "but he couldn't function without a harem. I could have stood that, maybe, but when he didn't mind if I made it with some other guy, too, I knew I didn't want that kind of life."

I looked at her in the mirror as I applied my lipstick. She had been hurt, and badly. She shook right down to her naked soul. So she was dropping down a social notch, according to her scale of values, and trying to repair her damaged ego with a black brother.

"You gonna make it with Edwin?" she asked, as if we were college chums comparing dates.

"I'm not a one-night stand." My tone was frigid. That's another thing I can't stand about white people. Too familiar, because we're colored.

"I dig Gregory," she said, pushing her hair out of her eyes. "He's kind of rough, but who wouldn't be, the kind of life he's led."

"And what kind of life is that?" I asked.

"Didn't you know? His mother was a whore in an exclusive brothel for white men only. That was before, when the British owned the island."

"I take it you like rough men?" I asked.

"There's usually something gentle and lost underneath," she replied.

A white woman came out of the toilet and Glenda went in. Jesus, I thought, Gregory gentle? The woman walked to the basin, flung some water in the general direction of her hands, and left.

"Poor Daddy is having a fit," Glenda volunteered from the john, "but there's not much he can do about it. He's afraid I'll leave him again, and he gets lonely without me, so he just tags along and tries to keep me out of trouble."

"And he pays the bills?"

She answered with a laugh. "Why not? He's loaded."

Why not, I thought with bitterness. You white women have always managed to have your cake and eat it, too. The toilet flushed with a roar like Niagara Falls. I opened the door and went back to our table. Let Glenda find her way back alone.

Edwin pulled my chair out and brushed his lips across the nape of my neck as I sat down. He still had not danced with anyone else, and his apparent desire was flattering. For a moment, I considered it. That's what I really needed, wasn't it? To walk down the moonlit beach wrapped in his arms, making it to some pad to be made? It would be a delightful story to tell at bridge sessions. But I shook my head at him, and this time my smile was more sad than teasing.

Glenda came back and crawled over Gregory's legs to the seat beside him. The bastard. He made no pretense of being a gentleman. Suddenly, I didn't know which of them I disliked the most. Gregory winked at me. I don't know where he got the impression I was his conspirator, but I got up to dance with him.

"That Glenda," he grinned, "she's the one I was on the boat with last night. I banged her plenty, in the room right next to her father. We could hear him coughing to let us know he was awake, but he didn't come in."

He laughed like a naughty schoolboy, and I joined in. He was a nerveless bastard all right, and it served Glenda right that we were laughing at her. Who asked her to crash our party, anyway? That's when I got the idea to take Gregory away from her.

"You gonna bang her again tonight?" I asked, a new, teasing quality in my voice. "Or are you gonna find something better to do?" To help him get the message I rubbed bellies with him.

He couldn't believe this sudden turn of events. I could almost see him thinking. With one stroke he could slap Glenda down a peg and repay Edwin for beating his time with me on the beach that morning.

"You wanna come with me?" he asked, making sure of his quarry.

"What you got to offer?" I peered at him through half-closed lids.

"Big Bamboo," he sang, the title of a popular calypso. We both laughed.

I felt a heady excitement of impending danger as Gregory pulled me back to the table. The men paid the bill, and suddenly we were standing outside the club in the bright moonlight. Gregory deliberately uncurled Glenda's arm from his and took a step toward me. Looking at Edwin and nodding in my direction, he said, "She's coming with me. Any objections?"

Edwin inhaled a mouthful of smoke. His face was inscrutable. "You want to go with him?" he asked me quietly.

I avoided his eyes and nodded. "Yes."

He flipped the cigarette with contempt at my feet and lit another one. "Help yourself to the garbage," he said, and leaned back against the building, one leg braced behind him. The others suddenly stilled their chatter, sensing trouble.

I was holding Gregory's arm now, and I felt his muscles tense. "No," I said as he moved toward Edwin. "You've got what you want. Forget it."

Glenda was ungracious in defeat. "What about me?" she screamed. She stared from one black face to another, her glance lingering on Edwin. But he wasn't about to come to her aid and take Gregory's leavings.

"You can go home in a cab," Gregory said, pushing her

ahead of him and pulling me behind him to a taxi waiting at the curb.

Glenda broke from his grasp. "You bastard. Who in the hell do you think you are, King Solomon? You can't dump me like this." She raised her hands as if to strike Gregory on the chest, but he caught them before they landed.

"Careful, white girl," he said. His voice was low but ominous. She froze.

"But why," she whimpered, all hurt child now. "You liked me last night. I know you did. Why are you treating me like this?"

"I didn't bring you here"—his voice was pleasant again —"so don't be trailing me all over town. When I want you, I'll come to that damn boat and get you. Now get in that cab before I throw you in. I'll see you tomorrow night. Maybe."

"You go to hell." She eluded him and turned on me, asking with incredible innocence, "What did I ever do to you?" Then she was running past toward the beach, her sobs drifting back to haunt me like a forlorn melody.

What had she ever done to me? And what had I just done? In order to degrade her for the crime of being white, I had sunk to the gutter. Suddenly Glenda was just another woman, vulnerable and lonely, like me.

We were sick, sick, sick. All fucked up. I had thought only Gregory was hung up in his love-hate, black-white syndrome, decades of suppressed hatred having sickened his soul. But I was tainted, too. I had forgotten my own misery long enough to inflict it on another woman who was only trying to ease her loneliness by making it with a soul brother. Was I jealous because she was able to function as a woman where I couldn't, because she realized that a man is a man, color be damned, while I was crucified on my own, anti-white-man cross?

What if she were going black trying to repent for some

ancient Nordic sin? How else could she atone except with the gift of herself? And if some black brother wanted to help a chick off her lily-white pedestal, he was entitled to that freedom, and it was none of my damned business anyway.

"Let's go, baby," Gregory said, tucking my arm under his.

The black bastard. I didn't even like the ugly ape. I backed away from him. "Leave me alone," I screamed. "Goddamit, just leave me alone!"

For a moment, we were all frozen into an absurd fresco —Alison, Dorothy, and the two boys looking at me in shocked disbelief, Edwin hiding behind a nonchalant smokescreen, Gregory off balance and confused, reaching out toward me.

I moved first, toward Edwin, but I had slammed the door behind me. He laughed, a mirthless sound in the stillness. He knew. I had forsaken him, but at least not for Gregory.

Then I was running down the beach looking for Glenda, hot tears of shame burning my face. How could I have been such a bitch? But the white beach, shimmering in the moonlight, was empty. And once again, I was alone.

LOUISE MERIWETHER

"I was raised in New York, in Harlem, under what could be called 'mean' circumstances if we wish to be polite and avoid more descriptive language. My father was a house painter and my mother did domestic work. There were five of us children (I was the only girl), and my oldest brother and my father are now dead.

"My parents were born in South Carolina and were part of that vast black migration to the 'promised land' in search of a better way of life. I've been 'migrating' a good deal of my life, from Harlem to Washington, D.C.; to the Bronx; Omaha, Nebraska; St. Paul, Minnesota; Los Angeles, and back to New York again, carrying a little bit of Harlem with me wherever I went.

"After graduating from Central Commercial High School in New York, I went to work as a secretary. Subsequently I returned to school at night, in the mornings, at noon, and finally bagged a degree in English from New York University and a master's degree in journalism from the University of California.

"After eighteen years on the West Coast, I have discovered that you *can* 'come home again' and I now live in the Bronx. During my travels I have been a legal secretary, bookkeeper, real-estate saleswoman, newspaper reporter, and story analyst at Universal Studios. (I also once set up pins in a bowling alley.)

"After publication of my first novel, *Daddy Was a Number Runner*, I turned my attention to black history for the kindergarten set, recognizing that the deliberate omission of Blacks from American history has been damaging to the children of both races. It reinforces in one a feeling of inferiority and in the other a myth of superiority.

"*The Freedom Ship of Robert Smalls* (Prentice-Hall, 1971) relates to the hijacking of a Confederate gunboat by eight slaves during the Civil War. *The Heart Man* (Prentice-Hall, 1972) is a capsule of the life of Dr. Daniel Hale Williams, who performed the world's first successful heart surgery, in 1893. *Don't Take the Bus on Monday* (1973) is the abbreviated story of that gallant lady Rosa Parks.

"I was active in the civil rights movement, specifically with CORE in Los Angeles, and spent the summer of '65 toting guns for the Deacons in Bogalusa.

"For the past three years I have been deeply involved in

the dilemma of writing another, longer novel, which I
hope will be completed in '75."

—Louise Meriwether

The central character in Meriwether's *Daddy Was a
Number Runner* is twelve-year-old Francie Coffin, who
narrates the story and allows us to see the complex community of Harlem in the 1930s through her perceptions.
It is a threatening world, not only for Francie, who is subjected to repeated sexual assaults, but also for her whole
family. She watches each one—her father, mother, and
two brothers—slowly being destroyed by the cruel realities
of ghetto life.

Paule Marshall points out in her review of Meriwether's novel that the sexual indignities Francie is subjected to as she tries to get an extra soup bone or bun "are
symbolic of the collective and historical violation of black
women." Indeed, the collective and historical sense is evident in all of Meriwether's characters, particularly the
black women. In the story "The Thick End Is for Whipping" (which is a section from *Daddy Was a Number
Runner*) Meriwether shows Francie's mother in the role
the black woman has historically been forced to play in
the family: leaving her family to do domestic work, worry-
ing about her sons' and daughters' learning too much in
the streets, and that final indignity, facing the social welfare interviewer as she applies for relief. Francie's Mama
sits in front of the social worker apologetically burying her
pride and listens to a lecture on the importance of being
truthful and obeying the welfare laws. Francie looks at
her mother's face and wonders where she has seen that
look before. It is an ancient look, worn for years before
and years to come by those who stayed and took care.

That same collective and historical sense pervades
Meriwether's short story "That Girl from Creektown,"

especially the characterizations of the women. The main character, for example, Lonnie Lyttle, graduates from a Mississippi high school in the year 1964. She has worked hard to finish school so, as her Mama has preached to her, she *"won't have to wash out some white woman's drawers for twenty dollars a week,"* another collective and historical experience. This advice from a black mother to her daughter is reminiscent of Zora Neale Hurston's novel *Their Eyes Were Watching God* (1937), in which Nanny tells her granddaughter, Janie, "I wanted yuh to pick from a higher bush and a sweeter berry." But no one in Creektown, Mississippi, in 1964 will give a black woman a decent job, and eventually economic necessity demands that Lonnie help out at home. Pushed to her limit and not wanting to give up on life completely, Lonnie goes back to an old relationship with Daniel, an older, married man, and accepts money for her love-making, hoping to save enough to one day get to New Orleans. But she knows she has been defeated as she walks away clutching his money in her trembling fist.

In the story "A Happening in Barbados," which is included in this anthology, the main character is a black woman who has "clawed [her] way up from the slums of Harlem via night school," so that she can now wear Saks Fifth Avenue clothes and vacation in the West Indian islands. But in spite of these outward trappings of having "made it," the black woman narrator also carries history with her in the form of bitterness, and loneliness, and the pain that makes her unable to react with humanity to other human beings.

Writing about these "frail whirlwinds falling in scattered particles upon the ground," Alice Walker says of women like Lonnie and Francie:

> They waited for a day when the unknown thing that was in them would be made known; but

guessed, somehow in their darkness, that on the day
of their revelation they would be long dead . . . they
walked, and even ran, in slow motion. For they were
going nowhere immediate, and the future was not
yet within their grasp.*

In the intensity of their pain, Meriwether's characters
are like whirlwinds fighting and charging against the
odds. But their frailty lies in the fact that they have not
yet outlived history.

* "In Search of Our Mothers' Gardens: The Creativity of Black
Women in the South," in *Ms.*, 2 (May 1974), p. 66.

The Black Mother-Daughter
Conflict

My Man Bovanne

TONI CADE BAMBARA

Blind people got a hummin jones if you notice. Which is understandable completely once you been around one and notice what no eyes will force you into to see people, and you get past the first time, which seems to come out of nowhere, and it's like you in church again with fat-chest ladies and old gents gruntin a hum low in the throat to whatever the preacher be saying. Shakey Bee bottom lip all swole up with Sweet Peach and me explainin how come the sweet-potato bread was a dollar-quarter this time stead of dollar regular and he say uh hunh he understand, then he break into this *thizzin* kind of hum which is quiet, but fiercesome just the same, if you ain't ready for it. Which I wasn't. But I got used to it and the onliest time I had to say somethin bout it was when he was playin checkers on the stoop one time and he commenst to hummin quite churchy seem to me. So I says, "Look here Shakey Bee, I can't beat you and Jesus too." He stop.

So that's how come I asked My Man Bovanne to dance. He ain't my man mind you, just a nice ole gent from the block that we all know cause he fixes things and the kids like him. Or used to fore Black Power got hold their minds and mess em around till they can't be civil to ole folks. So we at this benefit for my niece's cousin who's runnin for somethin with this Black party somethin or other behind her. And I press up close to dance with Bovanne who blind and I'm hummin and he hummin, chest to chest like talkin. Not jammin my breasts into the man. Wasn't bout tits. Was bout vibrations. And he dug it and asked me what color dress I had on and how my hair was fixed and how I was doin without a man, not nosy but nice-like, and who was at this affair and was the canapés dainty-stingy or healthy enough to get hold of proper. Comfy and cheery is what I'm tryin to get across. Touch talkin like the heel of the hand on the tambourine or on a drum.

But right away Joe Lee come up on us and frown for dancin so close to the man. My own son who knows what kind of warm I am about; and don't grown men call me long distance and in the middle of the night for a little Mama comfort? But he frown. Which ain't right since Bovanne can't see and defend himself. Just a nice old man who fixes toasters and busted irons and bicycles and things and changes the lock on my door when my men friends get messy. Nice man. Which is not why they invited him. Grass roots you see. Me and Sister Taylor and the woman who does heads at Mamies and the man from the barber shop, we all there on account of we grass roots. And I ain't never been souther than Brooklyn Battery and no more country than the window box on my fire escape. And just yesterday my kids tellin me to take them countrified rags off my head and be cool. And now can't get Black enough to suit em. So everybody passin sayin My Man Bovanne. Big deal, keep steppin and don't even stop a minute to get the man a drink or one of them cute sandwiches or tell him what's goin on. And him standin there with a smile ready case someone do speak he want to be ready. So that's how come I pull him on the dance floor and we dance squeezin past the tables and chairs and all them coats and people standin round up in each other face talkin bout this and that but got no use for this blind man who mostly fixed skates and skooters for all these folks when they was just kids. So I'm pressed up close and we touch talkin with the hum. And here come my daughter cuttin her eye at me like she do when she tell me about my "apolitical" self like I got hoof and mouf disease and there ain't no hope at all. And I don't pay her no mind and just look up in Bovanne shadow face and tell him his stomach like a drum and he laugh. Laugh real loud. And here come my youngest, Task, with a tap on my elbow like he the third grade monitor and I'm cuttin up on the line to assembly.

"I was just talkin on the drums," I explained when they hauled me into the kitchen. I figured drums was my best defense. They can get ready for drums what with all this heritage business. And Bovanne stomach just like that drum Task give me when he come back from Africa. You just touch it and it hum thizzm, thizzm. So I stuck to the drum story. "Just drummin that's all."

"Mama, what are you talkin about?"

"She had too much to drink," say Elo to Task cause she don't hardly say nuthin to me direct no more since that ugly argument about my wigs.

"Look here Mama," say Task, the gentle one. "We just tryin to pull your coat. You were makin a spectacle of yourself out there dancing like that."

"Dancin like what?"

Task run a hand over his left ear like his father for the world and his father before that.

"Like a bitch in heat," say Elo.

"Well uhh, I was goin to say like one of them sex-starved ladies gettin on in years and not too discriminating. Know what I mean?"

I don't answer cause I'll cry. Terrible thing when your own children talk to you like that. Pullin me out the party and hustlin me into some stranger's kitchen in the back of a bar just like the damn police. And ain't like I'm old old. I can still wear me some sleeveless dresses without the meat hangin off my arm. And I keep up with some thangs through my kids. Who ain't kids no more. To hear them tell it. So I don't say nuthin.

"Dancin with that tom," say Elo to Joe Lee, who leanin on the folks' freezer. "His feet can smell a cracker a mile away and go into their shuffle number post haste. And them eyes. He could be a little considerate and put on some shades. Who wants to look into them blown-out fuses that—"

"Is this what they call the generation gap?" I say.

"Generation gap," spits Elo, like I suggested castor oil and fricassee possum in the milk-shakes or somethin. "That's a white concept for a white phenomenon. There's no generation gap among Black people. We are a col—"

"Yeh, well never mind," says Joe Lee. "The point is Mama . . . well, it's pride. You embarrass yourself and us too dancin like that."

"I wasn't shame." Then nobody say nuthin. Them standin there in they pretty clothes with drinks in they hands and gangin up on me, and me in the third-degree chair and nary a olive to my name. Felt just like the police got hold to me.

"First of all," Task say, holdin up his hand and tickin off the offenses, "the dress. Now that dress is too short, Mama, and too low-cut for a woman your age. And Tamu's going to make a speech tonight to kick off the campaign and will be introducin you and expecting you to organize the council of elders—"

"Me? Didn nobody ask me nuthin. You mean Nisi? She change her name?"

"Well, Norton was supposed to tell you about it. Nisi wants to introduce you and then encourage the older folks to form a Council of the Elders to act as an advisory—"

"And you going to be standing there with your boobs out and that wig on your head and that hem up to your ass. And people'll say, 'Ain't that the horny bitch that was grindin with the blind dude?'"

"Elo, be cool a minute," say Task, gettin to the next finger. "And then there's the drinkin. Mama, you know you can't drink cause next thing you know you be laughin loud and carryin on," and he grab another finger for the loudness. "And then there's the dancin. You been tattooed on the man for four records straight and slow draggin even on the fast number. How you think that look for a woman your age?"

"What's my age?"

"What?"

"I'm axin you all a simple question. You keep talkin bout what's proper for a woman my age. How old am I anyhow?" And Joe Lee slams his eyes shut and squinches up his face to figure. And Task run a hand over his ear and stare into his glass like the ice cubes goin calculate for him. And Elo just starin at the top of my head like she goin rip the wig off any minute now.

"Is your hair braided up under that thing? If so, why don't you take it off? You always did so a neat cornroll."

"Uh huh," cause I'm thinkin how she couldn't undo her hair fast enough talking bout cornroll so countrified. None of which was the subject. "How old, I say?"

"Sixtee-one or—"

"You a damn lie Joe Lee Peoples."

"And that's another thing," say Task on the fingers.

"You know what you all can kiss," I say, gettin up and brushin the wrinkles out my lap.

"Oh, Mama," Elo say, puttin a hand on my shoulder like she hasn't done since she left home and the hand landin light and not sure it supposed to be there. Which hurt me to my heart. Cause this was the child in our happiness fore Mr. Peoples die. And I carried that child strapped to my chest till she was nearly two. We was close is what I'm tryin to tell you. Cause it was more me in the child than the others. And even after Task it was the girlchild I covered in the night and wept over for no reason at all less it was she was a chub-chub like me and not very pretty, but a warm child. And how did things get to this, that she can't put a sure hand on me and say Mama we love you and care about you and you entitled to enjoy yourself cause you a good woman?

"And then there's Reverend Trent," say Task, glancin from left to right like they hatchin a plot and just now lettin me in on it. "You were suppose to be talking with him tonight, Mama, about giving us his basement for campaign headquarters and—"

"Didn nobody tell me nuthin. If grass roots mean you kept in the dark I can't use it. I really can't. And Reven Trent a fool anyway the way he tore into the widow man up there on Edgecomb cause he wouldn't take in three of them foster children and the woman not even comfy in the ground yet and the man's mind messed up and—"

"Look here," say Task. "What we need is a family conference so we can get all this stuff cleared up and laid out on the table. In the meantime I think we better get back into the other room and tend to business. And in the meantime, Mama, see if you can't get to Reverend Trent and—"

"You want me to belly rub with the Reven, that it?"

"Oh damn," Elo say and go through the swingin door.

"We'll talk about all this at dinner. How's tomorrow night, Joe Lee?" While Joe Lee being self-important I'm wonderin who's doin the cookin and how come no body ax me if I'm free and do I get a corsage and things like that. Then Joe nod that it's O.K. and he go through the swingin door and just a little hubbub come through from the other room. Then Task smile his smile, lookin just like his daddy and he leave. And it just me in this stran-

ger's kitchen, which was a mess I wouldn't never let my
kitchen look like. Poison you just to look at the pots. Then
the door swing the other way and it's My Man Bovanne
standin there sayin Miss Hazel but lookin at the deep fry
and then at the steam table, and most surprised when I
come up on him from the other direction and take him on
out of there. Pass the folks pushin up towards the stage
where Nisi and some other people settin and ready to talk,
and folks gettin to the last of the sandwiches and the
booze fore they settle down in one spot and listen serious.
And I'm thinkin bout tellin Bovanne what a lovely long
dress Nisi got on and the earrings and her hair piled up in
a cone and the people bout to hear how we all gettin
screwed and gotta form our own party and everybody
there listenin and lookin. But instead I just haul the man
on out of there, and Joe Lee and his wife look at me like
I'm terrible, but they ain't said boo to the man yet. Cause
he blind and old and don't nobody there need him since
they grown up and don't need they skates fixed no more.

"Where we goin, Miss Hazel?" Him knowin all the
time.

"First we gonna buy you some dark sunglasses. Then
you comin with me to the supermarket so I can pick up tomorrow's dinner, which is goin to be a grand thing
proper and you invited. Then we goin to my house."

"That be fine. I surely would like to rest my feet." Bein
cute, but you got to let men play out they little show,
blind or not. So he chat on bout how tired he is and how
he appreciate me takin him in hand this way. And I'm
thinkin I'll have him change the lock on my door first
thing. Then I'll give the man a nice warm bath with jas-
mine leaves in the water and a little Epsom salt on the
sponge to do his back. And then a good rubdown with
rose water and olive oil. Then a cup of lemon tea with a
taste in it. And a little talcum, some of that fancy stuff

Nisi mother sent over last Christmas. And then a massage, a good face massage round the forehead which is the worryin part. Cause you gots to take care of the older folks. And let them know they still needed to run the mimeo machine and keep the spark plugs clean and fix the mailboxes for folks who might help us get the breakfast program goin, and the school for the little kids and the campaign and all. Cause old folks is the nation. That what Nisi was sayin and I mean to do my part.

"I imagine you are a very pretty woman, Miss Hazel."

"I surely am," I say just like the hussy my daughter always say I was.

TONI CADE BAMBARA

Born and raised a New Yorker, Toni Cade Bambara grew up in Harlem and Bedford-Stuyvesant, where she attended public and private schools. She received a B.A. from Queens College in 1959 and an M.A. from the City College of New York in 1963. Her career experiences are many and varied, ranging from social investigator with the New York State Department of Welfare (1959–61) to community organizer, youth worker, settlement-house director, and free-lance writer. Since editing *The Black Woman*, a collection of essays, stories, and poems published in 1970, she has written *Tales and Stories for Black Folks* (1971) and a book of short stories, *Gorilla, My Love*, which was published in 1972. Currently, Ms. Bambara is artist-in-residence at a neighborhood arts center in Atlanta and is working on *Children of Struggle*, a series of political poems for children.

The central consciousness that runs through the stories in *Gorilla, My Love* is that of a young black girl, Hazel Elizabeth Deborah Parker. Her point of view is important, because Hazel is the kind of adolescent who is enough of her own person to pierce through the hypocrisy and pretentiousness of the adult world. The racism and sexism of that world are exposed through Hazel's eyes. In "The Lesson," for example, she and some other neighborhood children are taken by a militant black woman to the F. A. O. Schwarz toy store, where they see such things as a handcrafted sailboat that costs nearly two thousand dollars. In spite of her outward cockiness, Hazel is ashamed of the poverty that makes her an outsider in this world where toys cost more than her family spends for food all year. Hazel is a particularly vulnerable and sensitive narrator, because she does not fit into the neat little slots reserved for females: she runs track and is the fastest thing on two feet; she plays pool and hates organdy dresses, goes to college at fifteen, and rejects all the conventions of being feminine.

The character of Hazel Parker reflects Toni Bambara's continuing concern about all forms of oppression, but especially the socially contrived roles women are forced into. In an essay entitled "On the Issue of Roles," which appeared in her anthology *The Black Woman*, Ms. Bambara comments on the sexist conditioning she sees women in this society subjected to and its peculiar effect on black people:

> I have always, I think, opposed the stereotypic definitions of "masculine" and "feminine," not only because I thought it was a lot of merchandising nonsense, but rather because I always found the either/or implicit in those definitions antithetical to what I was all about—and what revolution for self is all about—the whole person. And I am beginning to see, especially lately—that the way those terms are generally defined and acted upon in this part of the world is a hindrance to full development. And that is a shame, for a revolutionary must be capable of, above all, total self-autonomy.

Everyday Use

ALICE WALKER

I will wait for her in the yard that Maggie and I made so clean and wavy yesterday afternoon. A yard like this is more comfortable than most people know. It is not just a yard. It is like an extended living room. When the hard clay is swept clean as a floor and the fine sand around the edges lined with tiny, irregular grooves, anyone can come and sit and look up into the elm tree and wait for the breezes that never come inside the house.

Maggie will be nervous until after her sister goes: she will stand hopelessly in corners, homely and ashamed of the burn scars down her arms and legs, eying her sister with a mixture of envy and awe. She thinks her sister has held life always in the palm of one hand, that "no" is a word the world never learned to say to her.

You've no doubt seen those TV shows where the child who has "made it" is confronted, as a surprise, by his own mother and father, tottering in weakly from backstage. (A pleasant surprise, of course: what would they do if parent and child came on the show only to curse out and insult each other?) On TV mother and child embrace and smile into each other's faces. Sometimes the mother and father weep, the child wraps them in his arms and leans across the table to tell how he would not have made it without their help. I have seen these programs.

Sometimes I dream a dream in which Dee and I are suddenly brought together on a TV program of this sort. Out of a dark and soft-seated limousine I am ushered into a bright room filled with many people. There I meet a smiling, gray, sporty man like Johnny Carson who shakes my hand and tells me what a fine girl I have. Then we are on the stage and Dee is embracing me with tears in her eyes. She pins on my dress a large orchid, even though she has told me once that she thinks orchids are tacky flowers.

In real life I am a large big-boned woman with rough, man-working hands. In the winter I wear flannel nightgowns to bed and overalls during the day. I can kill and clean a hog as mercilessly as a man. My fat keeps me hot in zero weather. I can work outside all day, breaking ice to get water for washing; I can eat pork liver cooked over the open fire minutes after it comes steaming from the hog. One winter I knocked a bull calf straight in the brain between the eyes with a sledgehammer and had the meat hung up to chill before nightfall. But of course all this does not show on television. I am the way my daughter would want me to be; a hundred pounds lighter, my skin like an uncooked barley pancake. My hair glistens in the hot bright lights. Johnny Carson has much to do to keep up with my quick and witty tongue.

But that is a mistake. I know even before I wake up. Who ever knew a Johnson with a quick tongue? Who can even imagine me looking a strange white man in the eye? It seems to me I have talked to them always with one foot raised in flight, with my head turned in whichever way is farthest from them. Dee, though. She would always look anyone in the eye. Hesitation was no part of her nature.

"How do I look, Mama?" Maggie says, showing just enough of her thin body enveloped in pink skirt and red blouse for me to know she's there almost hidden by the door.

"Come out into the yard," I say.

Have you ever seen a lame animal, perhaps a dog run over by some careless person rich enough to own a car, sidle up to someone who is ignorant enough to be kind to him? That is the way my Maggie walks. She has been like this, chin on chest, eyes on ground, feet in shuffle, ever since the fire that burned the other house to the ground.

Dee is lighter than Maggie, with nicer hair and a fuller figure. She's a woman now, though sometimes I forget. How long ago was it that the other house burned? Ten, twelve years? Sometimes I can still hear the flames and feel Maggie's arms sticking to me, her hair smoking and her dress falling off her in little black papery flakes. Her eyes seemed stretched open, blazed open by the flames reflected in them. And Dee. I see her standing off under the sweetgum tree she used to dig gum out of; a look of concentration on her face as she watched the last dingy gray board of the house fall in toward the red-hot brick chimney. Why don't you do a dance around the ashes? I'd wanted to ask her. She had hated the house that much.

I used to think she hated Maggie too. But that was before we raised the money, the church and me, to send her to Augusta to school. She used to read to us without pity; forcing words, lies, other folks' habits, whole lives upon us two, sitting trapped and ignorant underneath her voice. She washed us in a river of make-believe, burned us with a lot of knowledge we didn't necessarily need to know. Pressed us to her with the serious way she read, to shove us away, like dimwits, at just the moment we seemed about to understand.

Dee wanted nice things. A yellow organdy dress to wear to her graduation from high school; black pumps to match a green suit she'd made from an old suit somebody gave me. She was determined to stare down any disaster in her efforts. Her eyelids would not flicker for minutes at a time. Often I fought off the temptation to shake her. At sixteen she had a style of her own: and knew what style was.

I never had an education myself. After second grade the school was closed down. Don't ask me why: in 1927 colored asked fewer questions than they do now. Sometimes Maggie reads to me. She stumbles along good-naturedly but can't see well. She knows she is not bright. Like good looks and money, quickness passed her by. She will marry John Thomas (who has mossy teeth in an earnest face), and then I'll be free to sit here and I guess just sing church songs to myself. Although I never was a good singer. Never could carry a tune. I was always better at a man's job. I used to love to milk till I was hooked in the side in '49. Cows are soothing and slow and don't bother you, unless you try to milk them the wrong way.

I have deliberately turned my back on the house. It is three rooms, just like the one that burned, except the roof is tin; they don't make shingle roofs anymore. There are no real windows, just some holes cut in the sides, like the portholes in a ship, but not round and not square, with rawhide holding the shutters up on the outside. This house is in a pasture too, like the other one. No doubt when Dee sees it she will want to tear it down. She wrote me once that no matter where we "choose" to live, she will manage to come see us. But she will never bring her friends. Maggie and I thought about this and Maggie asked me, "Mama, when did Dee ever *have* any friends?"

She had a few. Furtive boys in pink shirts hanging about on washday after school. Nervous girls who never laughed. Impressed with her, they worshiped the well-turned phrase, the cute shape, the scalding humor that erupted like bubbles in lye. She read to them.

When she was courting Jimmy T she didn't have much time to pay to us, but turned all her fault-finding power on him. He *flew* to marry a cheap city girl from a family of ignorant, flashy people. She hardly had time to recompose herself.

When she comes I will meet . . . but there they are!

Maggie attempts to make a dash for the house, in her shuffling way, but I stay her with my hand. "Come back here," I say. And she stops and tries to dig a well in the sand with her toe.

It is hard to see them clearly through the strong sun. But even the first glimpse of leg out of the car tells me it is Dee. Her feet were always neat looking, as if God himself had shaped them with a certain style. From the other side of the car comes a short, stocky man. Hair is all over his head a foot long and hanging from his chin like a kinky mule tail. I hear Maggie suck in her breath. "Uhnnnh," is what it sounds like. Like when you see the wriggling end of a snake just in front of your foot on a road. "Uhnnnh."

Dee, next. A dress down to the ground, in this hot weather. A dress so loud it hurts my eyes. There are yellows and oranges enough to throw back the light of the sun. I feel my whole face warming from the heat waves it throws out. Earrings gold too, and hanging down to her shoulders. Bracelets dangling and making noises when she moves her arm up to shake the folds of the dress out of her armpits. The dress is loose and flows, and as she walks closer, I like it. I hear Maggie go "Uhnnnh" again. It is her sister's hair. It stands straight up like the wool on a sheep. It is black as night and around the edges are two long pigtails that rope about like small lizards disappearing behind her ears.

"Wa-su-zo-Tean-o!" she says, coming on in that gliding way the dress makes her move. The short stocky fellow with the hair to his navel is all grinning and he follows up with, "Asalamalakim, my mother and sister!" He moves to hug Maggie but she falls back, right up against the back of my chair. I feel her trembling there, and when I look up I see the perspiration falling off her skin.

"Don't get up," says Dee. Since I am stout it takes something of a push. You can see me trying to move a second or two before I make it. She turns, showing white heels through her sandals, and goes back to the car. Out she peeks next with a Polaroid. She stoops down quickly and snaps off picture after picture of me sitting there in front of the house with Maggie cowering behind me. She never takes a shot without making sure the house is included. When a cow comes nibbling around the edge of the yard she snaps it and me and Maggie *and* the house. Then she puts the Polaroid on the back seat of the car, and comes up and kisses me on the forehead.

Meanwhile Asalamalakim is going through motions with Maggie's hand. Maggie's hand is as limp as a fish, and probably as cold, despite the sweat, and she keeps trying to pull it back. It looks like Asalamalakim wants to shake hands but wants to do it fancy. Or maybe he don't know how people shake hands. Anyhow, he soon gives up on Maggie.

"Well," I say. "Dee."

"No, Mama," she says. "Not 'Dee,' Wangero Lee-wanika Kemanjo!"

"What happened to 'Dee'?" I wanted to know.

"She's dead," Wangero said. "I couldn't bear it any longer, being named after the people who oppress me."

"You know well as me you was named after your aunt Dicie," I said. Dicie is my sister. She named Dee. We called her "Big Dee" after Dee was born.

"But who was *she* named after?" asked Wangero.

"I guess after Grandma Dee," I said.

"And who was she named after?" asked Wangero.

"Her mother," I said, and saw Wangero was getting tired. "That's about as far back as I can trace it," I said. Though, in fact, I probably could have carried it back beyond the Civil War through the branches.

"Well," said Asalamalakim, "there you are."

"Uhnnnh," I heard Maggie say.

"There I was not," I said, "before 'Dicie' cropped up in our family, so why should I try to trace it that far back?"

He just stood there grinning, looking down on me like somebody inspecting a Model A car. Every once in a while he and Wangero sent eye signals over my head.

"How do you pronounce this name?" I asked.

"You don't have to call me by it if you don't want to," said Wangero.

"Why shouldn't I?" I asked. "If that's what you want us to call you, we'll call you."

"I know it might sound awkward at first," said Wangero.

"I'll get used to it," I said. "Ream it out again."

Well, soon we got the name out of the way. Asalamalakim had a name twice as long and three times as hard. After I tripped over it two or three times he told me to just call him Hakim-a-barber. I wanted to ask him was he a barber, but I didn't really think he was, so I didn't ask.

"You must belong to those beef-cattle peoples down the road," I said. They said "Asalamalakim" when they met you too, but they didn't shake hands. Always too busy: feeding the cattle, fixing the fences, putting up salt-lick shelters, throwing down hay. When the white folks poisoned some of the herd, the men stayed up all night with rifles in their hands. I walked a mile and a half just to see the sight.

Hakim-a-barber said, "I accept some of their doctrines, but farming and raising cattle is not my style." They didn't tell me, and I didn't ask, whether Wangero (Dee) had really gone and married him.

We sat down to eat and right away he said he didn't eat collards and pork was unclean. Wangero, though, went on through the chitlins and corn bread, the greens and everything else. She talked a blue streak over the sweet potatoes. Everything delighted her. Even the fact that we still used the benches her daddy made for the table when we couldn't afford to buy chairs.

"Oh, Mama!" she cried. Then turned to Hakim-a-barber. "I never knew how lovely these benches are. You can feel the rump prints," she said, running her hands underneath her and along the bench. Then she gave a sigh and her hand closed over Grandma Dee's butter dish. "That's it!" she said. "I knew there was something I wanted to ask you if I could have." She jumped up from the table and went over in the corner where the churn stood, the milk in it clabber by now. She looked at the churn and looked at it.

"This churn top is what I need," she said. "Didn't Uncle Buddy whittle it out of a tree you all used to have?"

"Yes," I said.

"Uh huh," she said happily. "And I want the dasher too."

"Uncle Buddy whittle that too?" asked the barber.

Dee (Wangero) looked up at me.

"Aunt Dee's first husband whittled the dash," said Maggie so low you almost couldn't hear her. "His name was Henry, but they called him Stash."

"Maggie's brain is like an elephant's," Wangero said, laughing. "I can use the churn top as a centerpiece for the alcove table," she said, sliding a plate over the churn, "and I'll think of something artistic to do with the dasher."

When she finished wrapping the dasher the handle stuck out. I took it for a moment in my hands. You didn't even have to look close to see where hands pushing the dasher up and down to make butter had left a kind of sink in the wood. In fact, there were a lot of small sinks; you could see where thumbs and fingers had sunk into the wood. It was beautiful light yellow wood, from a tree that grew in the yard where Big Dee and Stash had lived.

After dinner Dee (Wangero) went to the trunk at the foot of my bed and started rifling through it. Maggie hung back in the kitchen over the dishpan. Out came Wangero with two quilts. They had been pieced by Grandma Dee, and then Big Dee and me had hung them on the quilt frames on the front porch and quilted them. One was in the Lone Star pattern. The other was Walk Around the Mountain. In both of them were scraps of dresses Grandma Dee had worn fifty and more years ago. Bits and pieces of Grandpa Jarrell's paisley shirts. And one teeny faded blue piece, about the size of a penny matchbox, that was from Great Grandpa Ezra's uniform that he wore in the Civil War.

"Mama," Wangero said sweet as a bird. "Can I have these old quilts?"

I heard something fall in the kitchen, and a minute later the kitchen door slammed.

"Why don't you take one or two of the others?" I asked. "These old things was just done by me and Big Dee from some tops your grandma pieced before she died."

"No," said Wangero. "I don't want those. They are stitched around the borders by machine."

"That'll make them last better," I said.

"That's not the point," said Wangero. "These are all pieces of dresses Grandma used to wear. She did all this stitching by hand. Imagine!" She held the quilts securely in her arms, stroking them.

"Some of the pieces, like those lavender ones, come from old clothes her mother handed down to her," I said, moving up to touch the quilts. Dee (Wangero) moved back just enough so that I couldn't reach the quilts. They already belonged to her.

"Imagine!" she breathed again, clutching them closely to her bosom.

"The truth is," I said, "I promised to give them quilts to Maggie, for when she marries John Thomas."

She gasped, like a bee had stung her.

"Maggie can't appreciate these quilts!" she said. "She'd probably be backward enough to put them to everyday use."

"I reckon she would," I said. "God knows I been saving 'em for long enough with nobody using 'em. I hope she will!" I didn't want to bring up how I had offered Dee (Wangero) a quilt when she went away to college. Then she had told me they were old-fashioned, out of style.

"But they're *priceless!*" she was saying now, furiously; for she has a temper. "Maggie would put them on the bed and in five years they'd be in rags. Less than that!"

"She can always make some more," I said. "Maggie knows how to quilt."

Dee (Wangero) looked at me with hatred. "You just will not understand. The point is these quilts, *these* quilts!"

"Well," I said, stumped, "what would *you* do with them?"

"Hang them," she said. As if that was the only thing you *could* do with quilts.

Maggie, by now, was standing in the door. I could almost hear the sound her feet made as they scraped over each other.

"She can have them, Mama," she said, like somebody used to never winning anything, or having anything reserved for her. "I can 'member Grandma Dee without the quilts."

I looked at her hard. She had filled her bottom lip with checkerberry snuff, and it gave her face a kind of dopey, hangdog look. It was Grandma Dee and Big Dee who taught her how to quilt herself. She stood there with her scarred hands hidden in the folds of her skirt. She looked at her sister with something like fear, but she wasn't mad at her. This was Maggie's portion. This was the way she knew God to work.

When I looked at her like that something hit me in the top of my head and ran down to the soles of my feet. Just like when I'm in church and the spirit of God touches me and I get happy and shout. I did something I never had done before: hugged Maggie to me, then dragged her on into the room, snatched the quilts out of Miss Wangero's hands and dumped them into Maggie's lap. Maggie just sat there on my bed with her mouth open.

"Take one or two of the others," I said to Dee.

But she turned without a word and went out to Hakim-a-barber.

"You just don't understand," she said, as Maggie and I came out to the car.

"What don't I understand?" I wanted to know.

"Your heritage," she said. And then she turned to Maggie, kissed her, and said, "You ought to try to make something of yourself too, Maggie. It's really a new day for us. But from the way you and Mama still live you'd never know it."

She put on some sunglasses that hid everything above the tip of her nose and her chin.

Maggie smiled; maybe at the sunglasses. But a real smile, not scared. After we watched the car dust settle I asked Maggie to bring me a dip of snuff. And then the two of us sat there just enjoying, until it was time to go in the house and go to bed.

ALICE WALKER

Born in Eatonton, Georgia, in 1944, the eighth child of
sharecropping parents, Alice Walker attended local
schools, then Spelman College in Atlanta, and graduated
from Sarah Lawrence in 1965, where she studied philosophy, literature, and history. She worked with voter regis-
tration in Georgia and on Head Start in Mississippi. As a
result of this experience, she describes the civil rights
struggles as a movement that awakened her to hope and
gave her life. She has published two volumes of poetry,
entitled *Once* (1968) and *Revolutionary Petunias*
(1973); a novel, *The Third Life of Grange Copeland*
(1970); a book of short stories, *In Love and Trouble*
(1973); a children's book, *Langston Hughes* (1974), and
many essays. After teaching and living in Mississippi for
several years, Ms. Walker now lives in New York, where
she is a fiction editor at *Ms.* magazine and is working on
a new novel about women who came of age during the
sixties.

In *Interviews with Black Writers*, Walker explains that
her preoccupations as a writer are with the spiritual sur-
vival of black people, but beyond that, she is committed to
"exploring the oppressions, the insanities, the loyalties,
and the triumphs of black women." Many of her black
women characters suffer or die tragically, but Walker sees
that cycle of destruction coming to an end as black
women, both in literature and in life, help to create a
place for the next generation of women to move into. But
perhaps more than anything else, Alice Walker is a black
southern writer, keenly aware of and sensitive to her black
southern roots, because, as she puts it, "the grace with
which we embrace life . . . is always a measure of what
has gone before." In her second book of poetry, *Revolu-*

tionary Petunias, she celebrates her memories of rural Georgia, where she grew up, where she experienced black community and family life and grew to understand that the traditions growing out of those rich experiences reveal the strength and resourcefulness of a people. In her treatment of the South, she is in the tradition of Zora Neale Hurston, Jean Toomer, and Ernest Gaines, who utilize the rituals and folklore of the black South as primary shaping forces in their work.

The Black Woman and
the Disappointment of
Romantic Love

SEEMOTHERMOTHERISVERY NICE

TONI MORRISON

The easiest thing to do would be to build a case out of her
foot. That is what she herself did. But to find out the
truth about how dreams die, one should never take the
word of the dreamer. The end of her lovely beginning was
probably the cavity in one of her front teeth. She
preferred, however, to think always of her foot. Although
she was the ninth of eleven children and lived on a ridge
of red Alabama clay seven miles from the nearest road, the
complete indifference with which a rusty nail was met
when it punched clear through her foot during her second
year of life saved Pauline Williams from total anonymity.
The wound left her with a crooked, archless foot that
flopped when she walked—not a limp that would have
eventually twisted her spine, but a way of lifting the bad
foot as though she were extracting it from little whirlpools
that threatened to pull it under. Slight as it was, this de-
formity explained for her many things that would have
been otherwise incomprehensible: why she alone of all
the children had no nickname; why there were no funny
jokes and anecdotes about funny things she had done;
why no one ever remarked on her food preferences—no
saving of the wing or neck for her—no cooking of the peas
in a separate pot without rice because she did not like rice;
why nobody teased her; why she never felt at home any-

where, or that she belonged anyplace. Her general feeling of separateness and unworthiness she blamed on her foot. Restricted, as a child, to this cocoon of her family's spinning, she cultivated quiet and private pleasures. She liked, most of all, to arrange things. To line things up in rows—jars on shelves at canning, peach pits on the step, sticks, stones, leaves—and the members of her family let these arrangements be. When by some accident somebody scattered her rows, they always stopped to retrieve them for her, and she was never angry, for it gave her a chance to rearrange them again. Whatever portable plurality she found, she organized into neat lines, according to their size, shape, or gradations of color. Just as she would never align a pine needle with the leaf of a cottonwood tree, she would never put the jars of tomatoes next to the green beans. During all of her four years of going to school, she was enchanted by numbers and depressed by words. She missed—without knowing what she missed—paints and crayons.

Near the beginning of World War I, the Williamses discovered, from returning neighbors and kin, the possibility of living better in another place. In shifts, lots, batches, mixed in with other families, they migrated, in six months and four journeys, to Kentucky, where there were mines and millwork.

"When all us left from down home and was waiting down by the depot for the truck, it was nighttime. June bugs was shooting everywhere. They lighted up a tree leaf, and I seen a streak of green every now and again. That was the last time I seen real june bugs. These things up here ain't june bugs. They's something else. Folks here call them fireflies. Down home they was different. But I recollect that streak of green. I recollect it well."

In Kentucky they lived in a real town, ten to fifteen houses on a single street, with water piped right into the kitchen. Ada and Fowler Williams found a five-room frame house for their family. The yard was bounded by a once-white fence against which Pauline's mother planted flowers and within which they kept a few chickens. Some of her brothers joined the Army, one sister died, and two got married, increasing the living space and giving the entire Kentucky venture a feel of luxury. The relocation was especially comfortable to Pauline, who was old enough to leave school. Mrs. Williams got a job cleaning and cooking for a white minister on the other side of town, and Pauline, now the oldest girl at home, took over the care of the house. She kept the fence in repair, pulling the pointed stakes erect, securing them with bits of wire, collected eggs, swept, cooked, washed, and minded the two younger children—a pair of twins called Chicken and Pie, who were still in school. She was not only good at housekeeping, she enjoyed it. After her parents left for work and the other children were at school or in mines, the house was quiet. The stillness and isolation both calmed and energized her. She could arrange and clean without interruption until two o'clock, when Chicken and Pie came home.

When the war ended and the twins were ten years old, they too left school to work. Pauline was fifteen, still keeping house, but with less enthusiasm. Fantasies about men and love and touching were drawing her mind and hands away from her work. Changes in weather began to affect her, as did certain sights and sounds. These feelings translated themselves to her in extreme melancholy. She thought of the death of newborn things, lonely roads, and strangers who appear out of nowhere simply to hold one's hand, woods in which the sun was always setting. In church especially did these dreams grow. The songs caressed her, and while she tried to hold her mind on the wages of sin, her body trembled for redemption, salvation, a mysterious rebirth that would simply happen, with no effort on her part. In none of her fantasies was she ever aggressive; she was usually idling by the riverbank, or gathering berries in a field when a someone appeared, with gentle and penetrating eyes, who—with no exchange of words—understood; and before whose glance her foot straightened and her eyes dropped. The someone had no face, no form, no voice, no odor. He was a simple Presence, an all-embracing tenderness with strength and a promise of rest. It did not matter that she had no idea of what to do or say to the Presence—after the wordless knowing and the soundless touching, her dreams disintegrated. But the Presence would know what to do. She had only to lay her head on his chest and he would lead her away to the sea, to the city, to the woods . . . forever.

There was a woman named Ivy who seemed to hold in her mouth all of the sounds of Pauline's soul. Standing a little apart from the choir, Ivy sang the dark sweetness that Pauline could not name; she sang the death-defying death that Pauline yearned for; she sang of the Stranger who *knew* . . .

> Precious Lord take my hand
> Lead me on, let me stand
> I am tired, I am weak, I am worn.
> Through the storms, through the night
> Lead me on to the light
> Take my hand, precious Lord, lead me on.
>
> When my way grows drear
> Precious Lord linger near,
> When my life is almost gone
> Hear my cry hear my call
> Hold my hand lest I fall
> Take my hand, precious Lord, lead me on.

Thus it was that when the Stranger, the someone, did appear out of nowhere, Pauline was grateful but not surprised.

He came, strutting right out of a Kentucky sun on the hottest day of the year. He came big, he came strong, he came with yellow eyes, flaring nostrils, and he came with his own music.

Pauline was leaning idly on the fence, her arms resting on the crossrail between the pickets. She had just put down some biscuit dough and was cleaning the flour from under her nails. Behind her at some distance she heard whistling. One of these rapid, high-note riffs that black boys make up as they go while sweeping, shoveling, or just walking along. A kind of city-street music where laughter belies anxiety, and joy is as short and straight as the blade of a pocketknife. She listened carefully to the music and let it pull her lips into a smile. The whistling got louder, and still she did not turn around, for she wanted it to last. While smiling to herself and holding fast to the break in somber thoughts, she felt something tickling her foot. She laughed aloud and turned to see. The whistler was bending down tickling her broken foot and kissing her leg. She could not stop her laughter—not until he looked up at her and she saw the Kentucky sun drenching the yellow, heavy-lidded eyes of Cholly Breedlove.

"When I first seed Cholly, I want you to know it was like all the bits of color from that time down home when all us chil'ren went berry picking after a funeral and I put some in the pocket of my Sunday dress, and they mashed up and stained my hips. My whole dress was messed with purple, and it never did wash out. Not the dress nor me. I could feel that purple deep inside me. And that lemonade Mama used to make when Pap

*came in out the fields. It be cool and yellowish, with
seeds floating near the bottom. And that streak of green
them june bugs made on the trees the night we left
from down home. All of them colors was in me. Just
sitting there. So when Cholly come up and tickled my
foot, it was like them berries, that lemonade, them
streaks of green the june bugs made, all come together.
Cholly was thin then, with real light eyes. He used to
whistle, and when I heerd him, shivers come on my skin."*

Pauline and Cholly loved each other. He seemed to
relish her company and even to enjoy her country ways
and lack of knowledge about city things. He talked with
her about her foot and asked, when they walked through
the town or in the fields, if she were tired. Instead of ig-
noring her infirmity, pretending it was not there, he made
it seem like something special and endearing. For the first
time Pauline felt that her bad foot was an asset.

And he did touch her, firmly but gently, just as she had
dreamed. But minus the gloom of setting suns and lonely
riverbanks. She was secure and grateful; he was kind and
lively. She had not known there was so much laughter in
the world.

They agreed to marry and go 'way up north, where
Cholly said steel mills were begging for workers. Young,
loving, and full of energy, they came to Lorain, Ohio.
Cholly found work in the steel mills right away, and
Pauline started keeping house.

And then she lost her front tooth. But there must have
been a speck, a brown speck easily mistaken for food but
which did not leave, which sat on the enamel for months,
and grew, until it cut into the surface and then to the
brown putty underneath, finally eating away to the root,
but avoiding the nerves, so its presence was not noticeable
or uncomfortable. Then the weakened roots, having

grown accustomed to the poison, responded one day to severe pressure, and the tooth fell free, leaving a ragged stump behind. But even before the little brown speck, there must have been the conditions, the setting that would allow it to exist in the first place.

In that young and growing Ohio town whose side streets, even, were paved with concrete, which sat on the edge of a calm blue lake, which boasted an affinity with Oberlin, the underground railroad station, just thirteen miles away, this melting pot on the lip of America facing the cold but receptive Canada—What could go wrong?

"Me and Cholly was getting along good then. We come up north; supposed to be more jobs and all. We moved into two rooms up over a furniture store, and I set about housekeeping. Cholly was working at the steel plant, and everything was looking good. I don't know what all happened. Everything changed. It was hard to get to know folks up here, and I missed my people. I weren't used to so much white folks. The ones I seed before was something hateful, but they didn't come around too much. I mean, we didn't have too much truck with them. Just now and then in the fields, or at the commissary. But they wa'nt all over us. Up north they was everywhere—next door, downstairs, all over the streets—and colored folks few and far between. Northern colored folk was different too. Dicty-like. No better than whites for meanness. They could make you feel just as no-count, 'cept I didn't expect it from them. That was the lonesomest time of my life. I 'member looking out them front windows just waiting for Cholly to come home at three o'clock. I didn't even have a cat to talk to."

In her loneliness, she turned to her husband for reassurance, entertainment, for things to fill the vacant places.

Housework was not enough; there were only two rooms, and no yard to keep or move about it. The women in the town wore high-heeled shoes, and when Pauline tried to wear them, they aggravated her shuffle into a pronounced limp. Cholly was kindness still, but began to resist her total dependence on him. They were beginning to have less and less to say to each other. He had no problem finding other people and other things to occupy him—men were always climbing the stairs asking for him, and he was happy to accompany them, leaving her alone.

Pauline felt uncomfortable with the few black women she met. They were amused by her because she did not straighten her hair. When she tried to make up her face as they did, it came off rather badly. Their goading glances and private snickers at her way of talking (saying "chil'ren") and dressing developed in her a desire for new clothes. When Cholly began to quarrel about the money she wanted, she decided to go to work. Taking jobs as a dayworker helped with the clothes, and even a few things for the apartment, but it did not help with Cholly. He was not pleased with her purchases and began to tell her so. Their marriage was shredded with quarrels. She was still no more than a girl, and still waiting for that plateau of happiness, that hand of a precious Lord who, when her way grew drear, would always linger near. Only, now she had a clearer idea of what drear meant. Money became the focus of all their discussions, hers for clothes, his for drink. The sad thing was that Pauline did not really care for clothes and makeup. She merely wanted other women to cast favorable glances her way.

After several months of doing daywork, she took a steady job in the home of a family of slender means and nervous, pretentious ways.

"Cholly commenced to getting meaner and meaner and wanted to fight me all of the time. I give him as good as I got. Had to. Look like working for that woman and fighting Cholly was all I did. Tiresome. But I holt on to my jobs, even though working for that woman was more than a notion. It wasn't so much her meanness as just simpleminded. Her whole family was. Couldn't get along with one another worth nothing. You'd think with a pretty house like that and all the money they could holt on to, they would enjoy one another. She haul off and cry over the leastest thing. If one of her friends cut her short on the telephone, she'd go to crying. She should of been glad she had a telephone. I ain't got one yet. I recollect oncet how her baby brother who she put through dentistry school didn't invite them to some big party he throwed. They was a big to-do about that. Everybody stayed on the telephone for days. Fussing and carrying on. She asked me, 'Pauline, what would you do if your own brother had a party and didn't invite you?' I said ifn I really wanted to go to that party, I reckoned I'd go anyhow. Never mind what he want. She just sucked her teeth a little and made out like what I said was dumb. All the while I was thinking how dumb she was. Whoever told her that her brother was her friend? Folks can't like folks just 'cause they has the same mama. I tried to like that woman myself. She was good about giving me stuff, but I just couldn't like her. Soon as I worked up a good feeling on her account, she'd do something ignorant and start in to telling me how to clean and do. If I left her on her own, she'd drown in dirt. I didn't have to pick up after Chicken and Pie the way I had to pick up after them. None of them knew so much as how to wipe their behinds. I know, 'cause I did the washing. And couldn't pee proper to save their lives. Her husband ain't hit the bowl yet.

Nasty white folks is about the nastiest things they is. But
I would have stayed on 'cepting for Cholly come over
by where I was working and cut up so. He come
there drunk wanting some money. When that white
woman see him, she turned red. She tried to act strong-
like, but she was scared bad. Anyway, she told Cholly
to get out or she would call the police. He cussed her and
started pulling on me. I would of gone upside his head,
but I don't want no dealings with the police. So I taken
my things and left. I tried to get back, but she didn't
want me no more if I was going to stay with Cholly.
She said she would let me stay if I left him. I thought
about that. But later on it didn't seem none too bright
for a black woman to leave a black man for a white
woman. She didn't never give me the eleven dollars she
owed me, neither. That hurt bad. The gas man had
cut the gas off, and I couldn't cook none. I really begged
that woman for my money. I went to see her. She
was mad as a wet hen. Kept on telling me I owed her for
uniforms and some old broken-down bed she give me.
I didn't know if I owed her or not, but I needed my
money. She wouldn't let up none, neither, even when I
give her my word that Cholly wouldn't come back there
no more. Then I got so desperate I asked her if she
would loan it to me. She was quiet for a spell, and then
she told me I shouldn't let a man take advantage over
me. That I should have more respect, and it was my
husband's duty to pay the bills, and if he couldn't, I
should leave and get alimony. All such simple stuff. What
was he gone give me alimony on? I seen she didn't
understand that all I needed from her was my eleven
dollars to pay the gas man so I could cook. She couldn't
get that one thing through her thick head. 'Are you
going to leave him, Pauline?' she kept on saying. I
thought she'd give me my money if I said I would, so I

said 'Yes, ma'am.' 'All right,' she said. 'You leave him, and
then come back to work, and we'll let bygones be
bygones.' 'Can I have my money today?' I said. 'No' she
said. 'Only when you leave him. I'm only thinking of
you and your future. What good is he, Pauline, what
good is he to you?' How you going to answer a woman
like that, who don't know what good a man is, and say
out of one side of her mouth she's thinking of your
future but won't give you your own money so you can
buy you something besides baloney to eat? So I said,
'No good, ma'am. He ain't no good to me. But just the
same, I think I'd best stay on.' She got up, and I left.
When I got outside, I felt pains in my crotch, I had held
my legs together so tight trying to make that woman
understand. But I reckon now she couldn't understand.
She married a man with a slash in his face instead of
a mouth. So how could she understand?"

One winter, Pauline discovered she was pregnant.
When she told Cholly, he surprised her by being pleased.
He began to drink less and come home more often. They
eased back into a relationship more like the early days of
their marriage, when he asked if she was tired or wanted
him to bring her something from the store. In this state of
ease, Pauline stopped doing daywork and returned to her
own housekeeping. But the loneliness in those two rooms
had not gone away. When the winter sun hit the peeling
green paint of the kitchen chairs, when the smoked hocks
were boiling in the pot, when all she could hear was the
truck delivering furniture downstairs, she thought about
back home, about how she had been all alone most of the
time then too, but that this lonesomeness was different.
Then she stopped staring at the green chairs, at the
delivery truck; she went to the movies instead. There in
the dark her memory was refreshed, and she succumbed to

her earlier dreams. Along with the idea of romantic love, she was introduced to another—physical beauty. Probably the most destructive ideas in the history of human thought. Both originated in envy, thrived in insecurity, and ended in disillusion. In equating physical beauty with virtue, she stripped her mind, bound it, and collected self-contempt by the heap. She forgot lust and simple caring for. She regarded love as possessive mating, and romance as the goal of the spirit. It would be for her a wellspring from which she would draw the most destructive emotions, deceiving the lover and seeking to imprison the beloved, curtailing freedom in every way.

She was never able, after her education in the movies, to look at a face and not assign it some category in the scale of absolute beauty, and the scale was one she absorbed in full from the silver screen. There at last were the darkened woods, the lonely roads, the riverbanks, the gentle, knowing eyes. There the flawed became whole, the blind sighted, and the lame and halt threw away their crutches. There death was dead, and people made every gesture in a cloud of music. There the black-and-white images came together, making a magnificent whole—all projected through the ray of light from above and behind.

It was really a simple pleasure, but she learned all there was to love and all there was to hate.

The onliest time I be happy seem like was when I was in the picture show. Every time I got, I went. I'd go early, before the show started. They'd cut off the lights, and everything be black. Then the screen would light up, and I'd move right on in them pictures. White men taking such good care of they women, and they all dressed up in big clean houses with the bathtubs right in the same room with the toilet. Them pictures gave me a lot of pleasure, but it made coming home hard, and

*looking at Cholly hard. I don't know. I 'member one time
I went to see Clark Gable and Jean Harlow. I fixed
my hair up like I'd seen hers on a magazine. A part on
the side, with one little curl on my forehead. It looked
just like her. Well, almost just like. Anyway, I sat in
that show with my hair done up that way and had a good
time. I thought I'd see it through to the end again, and
I got up to get me some candy. I was sitting back in my
seat, and I taken a big bite of that candy, and it pulled
a tooth right out of my mouth. I could of cried. I
had good teeth, not a rotten one in my head. I don't
believe I ever did get over that. There I was, five months
pregnant, trying to look like Jean Harlow, and a front
tooth gone. Everything went then. Look like I just
didn't care no more after that. I let my hair go back,
plaited it up, and settled down to just being ugly. I still
went to the pictures, though, but the meanness got worse.
I wanted my tooth back. Cholly poked fun at me,
and we started fighting again. I tried to kill him. He
didn't hit me too hard, 'cause I were pregnant I guess,
but the fights, once they got started up again, kept up.
He begin to make me madder than anything I knowed,
and I couldn't keep my hands off him. Well, I had that
baby—a boy—and after that got pregnant again with
another one. But it weren't like I thought it was gone be.
I loved them and all, I guess, but maybe it was having
no money, or maybe it was Cholly, but they sure worried
the life out of me. Sometimes I'd catch myself hollering
at them and beating them, and I'd feel sorry for
them, but I couldn't seem to stop. When I had the second
one, a girl, I 'member I said I'd love it no matter what it
looked like. She looked like a black ball of hair. I don't
recollect trying to get pregnant that first time. But
that second time, I actually tried to get pregnant. Maybe
'cause I'd had one already and wasn't scairt to do it.*

*Anyway, I felt good, and wasn't thinking on the carrying,
just the baby itself. I used to talk to it whilst it be still
in the womb. Like good friends we was. You know.
I be hanging wash and I knowed lifting weren't good
for it. I'd say to it holt on now I gone hang up these few
rags, don't get froggy; it be over soon. It wouldn't
leap or nothing. Or I be mixing something in a bowl for
the other chile and I'd talk to it then too. You know,
just friendly talk. On up til the end I felted good about
that baby. I went to the hospital when my time come.
So I could be easeful. I didn't want to have it at home
like I done with the boy. They put me in a big room with
a whole mess of women. The pains was coming, but not
too bad. A little old doctor come to examine me. He
had all sorts of stuff. He gloved his hand and put some
kind of jelly on it and rammed it up between my legs.
When he left off, some more doctors come. One old one
and some young ones. The old one was learning the
young ones about babies. Showing them how to do.
When he got to me he said now these here women you
don't have any trouble with. They deliver right away and
with no pain. Just like horses. The young ones smiled
a little. They looked at my stomach and between
my legs. They never said nothing to me. Only one looked
at me. Looked at my face, I mean. I looked right back at
him. He dropped his eyes and turned red. He knowed,
I reckon, that maybe I weren't no horse foaling. But
them others. They didn't know. They went on. I seed
them talking to them white women: 'How you feel?
Gonna have twins?' Just shucking them, of course, but
nice talk. Nice friendly talk. I got edgy, and when
them pains got harder, I was glad. Glad to have something
else to think about. I moaned something awful. The
pains wasn't as bad as I let on, but I had to let them
people know having a baby was more than a bowel*

movement. I hurt just like them white women. Just 'cause
I wasn't hooping and hollering before didn't mean
I wasn't feeling pain. What'd they think? That just
'cause I knowed how to have a baby with no fuss that
my behind wasn't pulling and aching like theirs? Besides,
that doctor don't know what he talking about. He
must never seed no mare foal. Who say they don't have
no pain? Just 'cause she don't cry? 'Cause she can't say
it, they think it ain't there? If they looks in her eyes
and see them eyeballs lolling back, see the sorrowful
look, they'd know. Anyways, the baby come. Big old
healthy thing. She looked different from what I thought.
Reckon I talked to it so much before I conjured up a
mind's eye view of it. So when I seed it, it was like
looking at a picture of your mama when she was a girl.
You knows who she is, but she don't look the same.
They give her to me for a nursing, and she liked to pull
my nipple off right away. She caught on fast. Not like
Sammy, he was the hardest child to feed. But Pecola
look like she knowed right off what to do. A right smart
baby she was. I used to like to watch her. You know
they makes them greedy sounds. Eyes all soft and wet.
A cross between a puppy and a dying man. But I
knowed she was ugly. Head full of pretty hair, but Lord
she was ugly."

When Sammy and Pecola were still young, Pauline
had to go back to work. She was older now, with no time
for dreams and movies. It was time to put all of the pieces
together, make coherence where before there had been
none. The children gave her this need; she herself was no
longer a child. So she became, and her process of becoming was like most of ours: she developed a hatred for
things that mystified or obstructed her; acquired virtues
that were easy to maintain; assigned herself a role in the

scheme of things; and harked back to simpler times for gratification.

She took on the full responsibility and recognition of breadwinner and returned to church. First, however, she moved out of the two rooms into a spacious first floor of a building that had been built as a store. She came into her own with the women who had despised her, by being more moral than they; she avenged herself on Cholly by forcing him to indulge in the weaknesses she despised. She joined a church where shouting was frowned upon, served on Stewardess Board No. 3, and became a member of Ladies Circle No. 1. At prayer meeting she moaned and sighed over Cholly's ways, and hoped God would help her keep the children from the sins of the father. She stopped saying "chil'ren" and said "childring" instead. She let another tooth fall, and was outraged by painted ladies who thought only of clothes and men. Holding Cholly as a model of sin and failure, she bore him like a crown of thorns, and her children like a cross.

It was her good fortune to find a permanent job in the home of a well-to-do family whose members were affectionate, appreciative, and generous. She looked at their houses, smelled their linen, touched their silk draperies, and loved all of it. The child's pink nightie, the stacks of white pillow slips edged with embroidery, the sheets with top hems picked out with blue cornflowers. She became what is known as an ideal servant, for such a role filled practically all of her needs. When she bathed the little Fisher girl, it was in a porcelain tub with silvery taps running infinite quantities of hot, clear water. She dried her in fluffy white towels and put her in cuddly night clothes. Then she brushed the yellow hair, enjoying the roll and slip of it between her fingers. No zinc tub, no buckets of stove-heated water, no flaky, stiff, grayish towels washed in a kitchen sink, dried in a dusty backyard, no tangled

black puffs of rough wool to comb. Soon she stopped trying to keep her own house. The things she could afford to
buy did not last, had no beauty or style, and were absorbed by the dingy storefront. More and more she
neglected her house, her children, her man—they were
like the afterthoughts one has just before sleep, the early-
morning and late-evening edges of her day, the dark edges
that made the daily life with the Fishers lighter, more delicate, more lovely. Here she could arrange things, clean
things, line things up in neat rows. Here her foot flopped
around on deep pile carpets, and there was no uneven
sound. Here she found beauty, order, cleanliness, and
praise. Mr. Fisher said, "I would rather sell her blueberry
cobblers than real estate." She reigned over cupboards
stacked high with food that would not be eaten for weeks,
even months; she was queen of canned vegetables bought
by the case, special fondants and ribbon candy curled up
in tiny silver dishes. The creditors and service people who
humiliated her when she went to them on her own behalf
respected her, were even intimidated by her, when she
spoke for the Fishers. She refused beef slightly dark or
with edges not properly trimmed. The slightly reeking
fish that she accepted for her own family she would all
but throw in the fishman's face if he sent it to the Fisher
house. Power, praise, and luxury were hers in this household. They even gave her what she had never had—a nickname—Polly. It was her pleasure to stand in her kitchen at
the end of a day and survey her handiwork. Knowing
there were soap bars by the dozen, bacon by the rasher,
and reveling in her shiny pots and pans and polished
floors. Hearing, "We'll never let her go. We could never
find anybody like Polly. She will *not* leave the kitchen
until everything is in order. Really, she is the ideal
servant."

Pauline kept this order, this beauty, for herself, a

private world, and never introduced it into her storefront, or to her children. Them she bent toward respectability, and in so doing taught them fear: fear of being clumsy, fear of being like their father, fear of not being loved by God, fear of madness like Cholly's mother's. Into her son she beat a loud desire to run away, and into her daughter she beat a fear of growing up, fear of other people, fear of life.

All the meaningfulness of her life was in her work. For her virtues were intact. She was an active church woman, did not drink, smoke, or carouse, defended herself mightily against Cholly, rose above him in every way, and felt she was fulfilling a mother's role conscientiously when she pointed out their father's faults to keep them from having them, or punished them when they showed any slovenliness, no matter how slight, when she worked twelve to sixteen hours a day to support them. And the world itself agreed with her.

It was only sometimes, sometimes, and then rarely, that she thought about the old days, or what her life had turned to. They were musings, idle thoughts, full sometimes of the old dreaminess, but not the kind of thing she cared to dwell on.

"I started to leave him once, but something came up. Once, after he tried to set the house on fire, I was all set in my mind to go. I can't even 'member now what held me. He sure ain't give me much of a life. But it wasn't all bad. Sometimes things wasn't all bad. He used to come easing into bed sometimes, not too drunk. I make out like I'm asleep, 'cause it's late, and he taken three dollars out of my pocketbook that morning or something. I hear him breathing, but I don't look around. I can see in my mind's eye his black arms thrown back behind his head, the muscles like great big peach stones

*sanded down, with veins running like little swollen
rivers down his arms. Without touching him I be feeling
those ridges on the tips of my fingers. I sees the palms
of his hands calloused to granite, and the long fingers
curled up and still. I think about the thick, knotty hair
on his chest, and the two big swells his breast muscles
make. I want to rub my face hard in his chest and feel
the hair cut my skin. I know just where the hair growth
slacks out—just above his navel—and how it picks up
again and spreads out. Maybe he'll shift a little, and his
leg will touch me, or I feel his flank just graze my
behind. I don't move even yet. Then he lift his head,
turn over, and put his hand on my waist. If I don't
move, he'll move his hand over to pull and knead my
stomach. Soft and slow-like. I still don't move, because
I don't want him to stop. I want to pretend sleep and
have him keep on rubbing my stomach. Then he will
lean his head down and bite my tit. Then I don't
want him to rub my stomach anymore. I want him to put
his hand between my legs. I pretend to wake up, and
turn to him, but not opening my legs. I want him to
open them for me. He does, and I be soft and wet where
his fingers are strong and hard. I be softer than I ever
been before. All my strength in his hand. My brain
curls up like wilted leaves. A funny, empty feeling is in
my hands. I want to grab holt of something, so I hold
his head. His mouth is under my chin. Then I don't
want his hand between my legs no more, because I
think I am softening away. I stretch my legs open, and he
is on top of me. Too heavy to hold, and too light not
to. He puts his thing in me. In me. In me. I wrap
my feet around his back so he can't get away. His face
is next to mine. The bed springs sounds like them crickets
used to back home. He puts his fingers in mine, and
we stretches our arms outwise like Jesus on the cross.*

*I hold on tight. My fingers and my feet hold on tight,
because everything else is going, going. I know he wants
me to come first. But I can't. Not until he does. Not
until I feel him loving me. Just me. Sinking into me.
Not until I know that my flesh is all that be on his mind.
That he couldn't stop if he had to. That he would
die rather than take his thing out of me. Of me. Not
until he has let go of all he has, and give it to me. To
me. To me. When he does, I feel a power. I be strong,
I be pretty, I be young. And then I wait. He shivers
and tosses his head. Now I be strong enough, pretty
enough, and young enough to let him make me come.
I take my fingers out of his and put my hands on his
behind. My legs drop back onto the bed. I don't make
no noise, because the chil'ren might hear. I begin to feel
those little bits of color floating up into me—deep in
me. That streak of green from the june-bug light, the
purple from the berries trickling along my thighs, Mama's
lemonade yellow runs sweet in me. Then I feel like
I'm laughing between my legs, and the laughing gets
all mixed up with the colors, and I'm afraid I'll come,
and afraid I won't. But I know I will. And I do.
And it be rainbow all inside. And it lasts and lasts and
lasts. I want to thank him, but don't know how, so
I pat him like you do a baby. He asks me if I'm all right.
I say yes. He gets off me and lies down to sleep. I want
to say something, but I don't. I don't want to take
my mind offen the rainbow. I should get up and go to the
toilet, but I don't. Besides, Cholly is asleep with his
leg throwed over me. I can't move and don't want to.*

"But it ain't like that anymore. Most times he's
thrashing away inside me before I'm woke, and through
when I am. The rest of the time I can't even be next
to his stinking drunk self. But I don't care 'bout it no
more. My Maker will take care of me. I know He will.

I know He will. Besides, it don't make no difference about this old earth. There is sure to be a glory. Only thing I miss sometimes is that rainbow. But like I say, I don't recollect it much anymore."

Reena

PAULE MARSHALL

Like most people with unpleasant childhoods, I am on
constant guard against the past—the past being for me the
people and places associated with the years I served out
my girlhood in Brooklyn. The places no longer matter
that much since most of them have vanished. The old
grammar school, for instance, P.S. 35 ("Dirty 5's" we
called it and with justification) has been replaced by a
low, coldly functional arrangement of glass and Perma-
stone which bears its name but has none of the feel of a
school about it. The small, grudgingly lighted stores along
Fulton Street, the soda parlor that was like a church with
its stained-glass panels in the door and marble floor have
given way to those impersonal emporiums, the super-
markets. Our house even, a brownstone relic whose halls
smelled comfortingly of dust and lemon oil, the somnolent
street upon which it stood, the tall, muscular trees which
shaded it were leveled years ago to make way for a city
housing project—a stark, graceless warren for the poor. So
that now whenever I revisit that old section of Brooklyn
and see these new and ugly forms, I feel nothing. I might
as well be in a strange city.

But it is another matter with the people of my past, the
faces that in their darkness were myriad reflections of
mine. Whenever I encounter them at the funeral or wake,
the wedding or christening—those ceremonies by which
the past reaffirms its hold—my guard drops and memories
banished to the rear of the mind rush forward to rout the

present. I almost become the child again—anxious and angry, disgracefully diffident.

Reena was one of the people from that time, and a main contributor to my sense of ineffectualness then. She had not done this deliberately. It was just that whenever she talked about herself (and this was not as often as most people) she seemed to be talking about me also. She ruthlessly analyzed herself, sparing herself nothing. Her honesty was so absolute it was a kind of cruelty.

She had not changed, I was to discover in meeting her again after a separation of twenty years. Nor had I really. For although the years had altered our positions (she was no longer the lord and I the lackey) and I could even afford to forgive her now, she still had the ability to disturb me profoundly by dredging to the surface those aspects of myself that I kept buried. This time, as I listened to her talk over the stretch of one long night, she made vivid without knowing it what is perhaps the most critical fact of my existence—that definition of me, of her and millions like us, formulated by others to serve out their fantasies, a definition we have to combat at an unconscionable cost to the self and even use, at times, in order to survive; the cause of so much shame and rage as well as, oddly enough, a source of pride: simply, what it has meant, what it means, to be a black woman in America.

We met—Reena and myself—at the funeral of her aunt who had been my godmother and whom I had also called aunt, Aunt Vi, and loved, for she and her house had been, respectively, a source of understanding and a place of calm for me as a child. Reena entered the church where the funeral service was being held as though she, not the minister, were coming to officiate, sat down among the immediate family up front, and turned to inspect those behind her. I saw her face then.

It was a good copy of the original. The familiar mold was there, that is, and the configuration of bone beneath the skin was the same despite the slight fleshiness I had never seen there before; her features had even retained their distinctive touches: the positive set to her mouth, the assertive lift to her nose, the same insistent, unsettling eyes which when she was angry became as black as her skin—and this was total, unnerving, and very beautiful. Yet something had happened to her face. It was different despite its sameness. Aging even while it remained enviably young. Time had sketched in, very lightly, the evidence of the twenty years.

As soon as the funeral service was over, I left, hurrying out of the church into the early November night. The wind, already at its winter strength, brought with it the smell of dead leaves and the image of Aunt Vi there in the church, as dead as the leaves—as well as the thought of Reena, whom I would see later at the wake.

Her real name had been Doreen, a standard for girls among West Indians (her mother, like my parents, was from Barbados), but she had changed it to Reena on her twelfth birthday—"As a present to myself"—and had enforced the change on her family by refusing to answer to the old name. "Reena. With two e's!" she would say and imprint those e's on your mind with the indelible black of her eyes and a thin threatening finger that was like a quill.

She and I had not been friends through our own choice. Rather, our mothers, who had known each other since childhood, had forced the relationship. And from the beginning, I had been at a disadvantage. For Reena, as early as the age of twelve, had had a quality that was unique, superior, and therefore dangerous. She seemed defined, even then, all of a piece, the raw edges of her adolescence smoothed over; indeed, she seemed to have es-

caped adolescence altogether and made one dazzling leap
from childhood into the very arena of adult life. At thirteen, for instance, she was reading Zola, Hauptmann,
Steinbeck, while I was still in the thrall of the Little
Minister and Lorna Doone. When I could only barely
conceive of the world beyond Brooklyn, she was talking of
the Civil War in Spain, lynchings in the South, Hitler in
Poland—and talking with the outrage and passion of a revolutionary. I would try, I remember, to console myself
with the thought that she was really an adult masquerad-
ing as a child, which meant that I could not possibly be
her match.

For her part, Reena put up with me and was, by turns,
patronizing and impatient. I merely served as the audience before whom she rehearsed her ideas and the yard-
stick by which she measured her worldliness and knowledge.

"Do you realize that this stupid country supplied Japan
with the scrap iron to make the weapons she's now using
against it?" she had shouted at me once.

I had not known that.

Just as she overwhelmed me, she overwhelmed her family, with the result that despite a half dozen brothers and
sisters who consumed quantities of bread and jam whenever they visited us, she behaved like an only child and
got away with it. Her father, a gentle man with skin the
color of dried tobacco and with the nose Reena had
inherited jutting out like a crag from his nondescript face,
had come from Georgia and was always making jokes
about having married a foreigner—Reena's mother being
from the West Indies. When not joking, he seemed
slightly bewildered by his large family and so in awe of
Reena that he avoided her. Reena's mother, a small, dry,
formidably black woman, was less a person to me than the
abstract principle of force, power, energy. She was alter-

nately strict and indulgent with Reena and, despite the inconsistency, surprisingly effective.

They lived when I knew them in a cold-water railroad flat above a kosher butcher on Belmont Avenue in Brownsville, some distance from us—and this in itself added to Reena's exotic quality. For it was a place where Sunday became Saturday, with all the stores open and pushcarts piled with vegetables and yard goods lined up along the curb, a crowded place where people hawked and spat freely in the streaming gutters and the men looked as if they had just stepped from the pages of the Old Testament with their profuse beards and long, black, satin coats.

When Reena was fifteen her family moved to Jamaica in Queens and since, in those days, Jamaica was considered too far away for visiting, our families lost contact and I did not see Reena again until we were both in college and then only once and not to speak to . . .

I had walked some distance and by the time I got to the wake, which was being held at Aunt Vi's house, it was well under way. It was a good wake. Aunt Vi would have been pleased. There was plenty to drink, and more than enough to eat, including some Barbadian favorites: coconut bread, pone made with the cassava root, and the little crisp codfish cakes that are so hot with peppers they bring tears to the eyes as you bite into them.

I had missed the beginning, when everyone had probably sat around talking about Aunt Vi and recalling the few events that had distinguished her otherwise undistinguished life. (Someone, I'm sure, had told of the time she had missed the excursion boat to Atlantic City and had held her own private picnic—complete with pigeon peas and rice and fricassee chicken—on the pier at 42nd Street.) By the time I arrived, though, it would have been indiscreet to mention her name, for by then the wake had become—and this would also have pleased her—a celebration of life.

I had had two drinks, one right after the other, and was well into my third when Reena, who must have been upstairs, entered the basement kitchen where I was. She saw me before I had quite seen her, and with a cry that alerted the entire room to her presence and charged the air with her special force, she rushed toward me.

"Hey, I'm the one who was supposed to be the writer, not you! Do you know, I still can't believe it," she said, stepping back, her blackness heightened by a white mocking smile. "I read both your books over and over again and I can't really believe it. My Little Paulie!"

I did not mind. For there was respect and even wonder behind the patronizing words and in her eyes. The old imbalance between us had ended and I was suddenly glad to see her.

I told her so and we both began talking at once, but Reena's voice overpowered mine, so that all I could do after a time was listen while she discussed my books, and dutifully answer her questions about my personal life.

"And what about you?" I said, almost brutally, at the first chance I got. "What've you been up to all this time?"

She got up abruptly. "Good Lord, in here's noisy as hell. Come on, let's go upstairs."

We got fresh drinks and went up to Aunt Vi's bedroom, where in the soft light from the lamps, the huge Victorian bed and the pink satin bedspread with roses of the same material strewn over its surface looked as if they had never been used. And, in a way, this was true. Aunt Vi had seldom slept in her bed or, for that matter, lived in her house, because in order to pay for it, she had had to work at a sleeping-in job which gave her only Thursdays and every other Sunday off.

Reena sat on the bed, crushing the roses, and I sat on one of the numerous trunks which crowded the room. They contained every dress, coat, hat, and shoe that Aunt Vi had worn since coming to the United States. I again asked Reena what she had been doing over the years.

"Do you want a blow-by-blow account?" she said. But despite the flippancy, she was suddenly serious. And when she began it was clear that she had written out the narrative in her mind many times. The words came too easily; the events, the incidents had been ordered in time, and the meaning of her behavior and of the people with whom she had been involved had been painstakingly analyzed. She talked willingly, with desperation almost. And the words by themselves weren't enough. She used her hands to give them form and urgency. I became totally involved with her and all that she said. So much so that as the night wore on I was not certain at times whether it was she or I speaking.

From the time her family moved to Jamaica until she was nineteen or so, Reena's life sounded, from what she told me in the beginning, as ordinary as mine and most of the girls we knew. After high school she had gone on to one of the free city colleges, where she had majored in journalism, worked part time in the school library, and, surprisingly enough, joined a houseplan. (Even I hadn't gone that far.) It was an all-Negro club, since there was a tacit understanding that Negro and white girls did not join each other's houseplans. "Integration, northern style," she said, shrugging.

It seems that Reena had had a purpose and a plan in joining the group. "I thought," she said with a wry smile, "I could get those girls up off their complacent rumps and out doing something about social issues. . . . I couldn't get them to budge. I remember after the war when a

Negro ex-soldier had his eyes gouged out by a bus driver down South I tried getting them to demonstrate on campus. I talked until I was hoarse, but to no avail. They were too busy planning the annual autumn frolic."

Her laugh was bitter but forgiving and it ended in a long, reflective silence. After which she said quietly, "It wasn't that they didn't give a damn. It was just, I suppose, that like most people they didn't want to get involved to the extent that they might have to stand up and be counted. If it ever came to that. Then another thing. They thought they were safe, special. After all, they had grown up in the North, most of them, and so had escaped the southern-style prejudice; their parents, like mine, were struggling to put them through college; they could look forward to being tidy little schoolteachers, social workers, and lab technicians. Oh, they were safe!" The sarcasm scored her voice and then abruptly gave way to pity. "Poor things, they weren't safe, you see, and would never be as long as millions like themselves in Harlem, on Chicago's South Side, down South, all over the place, were unsafe. I tried to tell them this—and they accused me of being oversensitive. They tried not to listen. But I would have held out and, I'm sure, even brought some of them around eventually if this other business with a silly boy hadn't happened at the same time. . . ."

Reena told me then about her first, brief, and apparently innocent affair with a boy she had met at one of the houseplan parties. It had ended, she said, when the boy's parents had met her. "That was it," she said and the flat of her hand cut into the air. "He was forbidden to see me. The reason? He couldn't bring himself to tell me, but I knew. I was too black.

"Naturally, it wasn't the first time something like that had happened. In fact, you might say that was the theme of my childhood. Because I was dark I was always being

plastered with Vaseline so I wouldn't look ashy. Whenever I had my picture taken they would pile a whitish
powder on my face and make the lights so bright I always
came out looking ghostly. My mother stopped speaking to
any number of people because they said I would have
been pretty if I hadn't been so dark. Like nearly every little black girl, I had my share of dreams of waking up to
find myself with long, blond curls, blue eyes, and skin like
milk. So I should have been prepared. Besides, that boy's
parents were really rejecting themselves in rejecting me.

"Take us"—and her hands, opening in front of my face
as she suddenly leaned forward, seemed to offer me the
whole of black humanity. "We live surrounded by white
images, and white in this world is synonymous with the
good, light, beauty, success, so that, despite ourselves
sometimes, we run after that whiteness and deny our
darkness, which has been made into the symbol of all that
is evil and inferior. I wasn't a person to that boy's parents,
but a symbol of the darkness they were in flight from, so
that just as they—that boy, his parents, those silly girls in
the houseplan—were running from me, I started running
from them . . ."

It must have been shortly after this happened when I saw
Reena at a debate which was being held at my college.
She did not see me, since she was one of the speakers and
I was merely part of her audience in the crowded auditorium. The topic had something to do with intellectual
freedom in the colleges (McCarthyism was coming into
vogue then) and aside from a Jewish boy from City
College, Reena was the most effective—sharp, provocative,
her position the most radical. The others on the panel
seemed intimidated not only by the strength and cogency
of her argument but by the sheer impact of her blackness
in their white midst.

Her color might have been a weapon she used to dazzle and disarm her opponents. And she had highlighted it with the clothes she was wearing: a white dress patterned with large blocks of primary colors I remember (it looked Mexican) and a pair of intricately wrought silver earrings —long and with many little parts which clashed like muted cymbals over the microphone each time she moved her head. She wore her hair cropped short like a boy's and it was not straightened like mine and the other Negro girls' in the audience, but left in its coarse natural state: a small forest under which her face emerged in its intense and startling handsomeness. I remember she left the auditorium in triumph that day, surrounded by a noisy entourage from her college—all of them white.

"We were very serious," she said now, describing the left-wing group she had belonged to then—and there was a defensiveness in her voice which sought to protect them from all censure. "We believed—because we were young, I suppose, and had nothing as yet to risk—that we could do something about the injustices which everyone around us seemed to take for granted. So we picketed and demonstrated and bombarded Washington with our protests, only to have our names added to the Attorney General's list for all our trouble. We were always standing on street corners handing out leaflets or getting people to sign petitions. We always seemed to pick the coldest days to do that." Her smile held long after the words had died.

"I, we all, had such a sense of purpose then," she said softly, and a sadness lay aslant the smile now, darkening it. "We were forever holding meetings, having endless discussions, arguing, shouting, theorizing. And we had fun. Those parties! There was always somebody with a guitar. We were always singing. . . ." Suddenly, she began singing—and her voice was sure, militant, and faintly self-mocking,

"But the banks are made of marble
With a guard at every door
And the vaults are stuffed with silver
That the workers sweated for . . ."

When she spoke again the words were a sad coda to the song. "Well, as you probably know, things came to an ugly head with McCarthy reigning in Washington, and I was one of the people temporarily suspended from school."

She broke off and we both waited, the ice in our glasses melted and the drinks gone flat.

"At first, I didn't mind," she said finally. "After all, we were right. The fact that they suspended us proved it. Besides, I was in the middle of an affair, a real one this time, and too busy with that to care about anything else." She paused again, frowning.

"He was white," she said quickly and glanced at me as though to surprise either shock or disapproval in my face. "We were very involved. At one point—I think just after we had been suspended and he started working—we even thought of getting married. Living in New York, moving in the crowd we did, we might have been able to manage it. But I couldn't. There were too many complex things going on beneath the surface," she said, her voice strained by the hopelessness she must have felt then, her hands shaping it in the air between us. "Neither one of us could really escape what our color had come to mean in this country. Let me explain. Bob was always, for some odd reason, talking about how much the Negro suffered, and although I would agree with him I would also try to get across that, you know, like all people we also had fun once in a while, loved our children, liked making love—that we were human beings, for God's sake. But he only wanted to hear about the suffering. It was as if this comforted him and eased his own suffering—and he did suffer because of any number of things: his own uncertainty, for one, his difficulties with his family, for another . . .

"Once, I remember, when his father came into New York, Bob insisted that I meet him. I don't know why I agreed to go with him. . . ." She took a deep breath and raised her head very high. "I'll never forget or forgive the look on that old man's face when he opened his hotel-room door and saw me. The horror. I might have been the personification of every evil in the world. His inability to believe that it was his son standing there holding my hand. His shock. I'm sure he never fully recovered. I know I never did. Nor can I forget Bob's laugh in the elevator afterwards, the way he kept repeating: 'Did you see his face when he saw you? Did you . . . ?' He had used me, you see. I had been the means, the instrument of his revenge.

"And I wasn't any better. I used him. I took every opportunity to treat him shabbily, trying, you see, through him, to get at that white world which had not only denied me, but had turned my own against me." Her eyes closed. "I went numb all over when I understood what we were doing to, and with, each other. I stayed numb for a long time."

As Reena described the events which followed—the break with Bob, her gradual withdrawal from the left-wing group ("I had had it with them too. I got tired of being 'their Negro,' their pet. Besides, they were just all talk, really. All theories and abstractions. I doubt that, with all their elaborate plans for the Negro and for the workers of the world, any of them had ever been near a factory or up to Harlem")—as she spoke about her rein-statement in school, her voice suggested the numbness she had felt then. It only stirred into life again when she talked of her graduation.

"You should have seen my parents. It was really their

day. My mother was so proud she complained about everything: her seat, the heat, the speaker; and my father just sat there long after everybody had left, too awed to move. God, it meant so much to them. It was as if I had made up for the generations his people had picked cotton in Georgia and my mother's family had cut cane in the West Indies. It frightened me."

I asked her after a long wait what she had done after graduating.

"How do you mean, what I did. Looked for a job. Tell me, have you ever looked for work in this man's city?"

"I know," I said, holding up my hand. "Don't tell me."

We both looked at my raised hand which sought to waive the discussion, then at each other and suddenly we laughed, a laugh so loud and violent with pain and outrage it brought tears.

"Girl," Reena said, the tears silver against her blackness. "You could put me blindfolded right now at the Times Building on 42nd Street and I would be able to find my way to every newspaper office in town. But tell me, how come white folks is so *hard?*"

"Just bo'n hard."

We were laughing again and this time I nearly slid off the trunk and Reena fell back among the satin roses.

"I didn't know there were so many ways of saying 'no' without ever once using the word," she said, the laughter lodged in her throat, but her eyes had gone hard. "Sometimes I'd find myself in the elevator, on my way out, and smiling all over myself because I thought I had gotten the job, before it would hit me that they had really said no, not yes. Some of those people in personnel had so perfected their smiles they looked almost genuine. The ones who used to get me, though, were those who tried to make the interview into an intimate chat between friends. They'd put you in a comfortable chair, offer you a cigarette, and order coffee. How I hated that coffee. They didn't know it—or maybe they did—but it was like offering me hemlock. . . .

"You think Christ had it tough?" Her laughter rushed against the air which resisted it. "I was crucified five days a week and half-day on Saturday. I became almost paranoid. I began to think there might be something other than color wrong with me which everybody but me could see, some rare disease that had turned me into a monster.

"My parents suffered. And that bothered me most, because I felt I had failed them. My father didn't say anything but I knew because he avoided me more than usual. He was ashamed, I think, that he hadn't been able, as a man and as my father, to prevent this. My mother—well, you know her. In one breath she would try to comfort me by cursing them: 'But Gor blind them,' "—and Reena's voice captured her mother's aggressive accent—" 'if you had come looking for a job mopping down their floors they would o' hire you, the brutes. But mark my words, their time goin' come, 'cause God don't love ugly and he ain't stuck on pretty . . .' And in the next breath she would curse me, 'Journalism! Journalism! Whoever heard of colored people taking up journalism. You must feel you's white or something so. The people is right to chuck you out their office. . . .' Poor thing, to make up for saying all that she would wash my white gloves every night and cook cereal for me in the morning as is I were a little girl again. Once she went out and bought me a suit she couldn't afford from Lord and Taylor's. I looked like a Smith girl in blackface in it. . . . So guess where I ended up?"

"As a social investigator for the Welfare Department. Where else?"

We were helpless with laughter again.

"You too?"

"No," I said, "I taught, but that was just as bad."

"No," she said, sobering abruptly. "Nothing's as bad as working for Welfare. Do you know what they really mean by a social investigator? A spy. Someone whose dirty job it is to snoop into the corners of the lives of the poor and make their poverty more vivid by taking from them the last shred of privacy. 'Mrs. Jones, is that a new dress you're wearing?' 'Mrs. Brown, this kerosene heater is not listed in the household items. Did you get an authorization for it?' 'Mrs. Smith, is that a telephone I hear ringing under the sofa?' I was utterly demoralized within a month.

"And another thing. I thought I knew about poverty. I mean, I remember, as a child, having to eat soup made with those white beans the government used to give out free for days running, sometimes, because there was nothing else. I had lived in Brownsville, among all the poor Jews and Poles and Irish there. But what I saw in Harlem, where I had my case load, was different somehow. Perhaps because it seemed so final. There didn't seem to be any way to escape from those dark hallways and dingy furnished rooms . . . All that defeat." Closing her eyes, she finished the stale whiskey and soda in her glass.

"I remember a client of mine, a girl my age with three children already and no father for them and living in the expensive squalor of a rooming house. Her bewilderment. Her resignation. Her anger. She could have pulled herself out of the mess she was in? People say that, you know, including some Negroes. But this girl didn't have a chance. She had been trapped from the day she was born in some small town down South.

"She became my reference. From then on and even now, whenever I hear people and groups coming up with all kinds of solutions to the quote Negro problem, I ask one question. What are they really doing for that girl, to save her or to save the children? . . . The answer isn't very encouraging."

It was some time before she continued, and then she told me that after Welfare she had gone to work for a private social-work agency, in their publicity department, and had started on her master's in journalism at Columbia. She also left home around this time.

"I had to. My mother started putting the pressure on me to get married. The hints, the remarks—and you know my mother was never the subtle type—her anxiety, which made me anxious about getting married after a while. Besides, it was time for me to be on my own."

In contrast to the unmistakably radical character of her late adolescence (her membership in the left-wing group, the affair with Bob, her suspension from college), Reena's life of this period sounded ordinary, standard—and she admitted it with a slightly self-deprecating, apologetic smile. It was similar to that of any number of unmarried professional Negro women in New York or Los Angeles or Washington: the job teaching or doing social work which brought in a fairly decent salary, the small apartment with kitchenette which they sometimes shared with a roommate; a car, some of them; membership in various political and social action organizations for the militant few like Reena; the vacations in Mexico, Europe, the West Indies, and now Africa; the occasional date. "The interesting men were invariably married," Reena said and then mentioned having had one affair during that time. She had found out he was married and had thought of her only as the perfect mistress. "The bastard," she said, but her smile forgave him.

"Women alone!" she cried, laughing sadly, and her raised opened arms, the empty glass she held in one hand made eloquent their aloneness. "Alone and lonely, and indulging themselves while they wait. The girls of the houseplan have reached their majority only to find that all those years they spent accumulating their degrees and finding the well-paying jobs in the hope that this would raise their stock have, instead, put them at a disadvantage. For the few eligible men around—those who are their intellectual and professional peers, whom they can respect (and there are very few of them)—don't necessarily marry them, but younger women without the degrees and the fat jobs, who are no threat, or they don't marry at all because they are either queer or mother-ridden. Or they marry white women. Now, intellectually I accept this. In fact, some of my best friends are white women . . ." And again our laughter—that loud, searing burst which we used to cauterize our hurt mounted into the unaccepting silence of the room. "After all, our goal is a fully integrated society. And perhaps, as some people believe, the only solution to the race problem is miscegenation. Besides, a man should be able to marry whomever he wishes. Emotionally, though, I am less kind and understanding, and I resent like hell the reasons some black men give for rejecting us for them."

"We're too middle-class-oriented," I said. "Conservative."

"Right. Even though, thank God, that doesn't apply to me."

"Too threatening . . . castrating . . ."

"Too independent and impatient with them for not being more ambitious . . . contemptuous . . ."

"Sexually inhibited and unimaginative . . ."

"And the old myth of the excessive sexuality of the black woman goes out the window," Reena cried.

"Not supportive, unwilling to submerge our interests for theirs . . ."

"Lacking in the subtle art of getting and keeping a man . . ."

We had recited the accusations in the form and tone of a litany, and in the silence which followed we shared a thin, hopeless smile.

"They condemn us," Reena said softly but with anger, "without taking history into account. We are still, most of us, the black woman who had to be almost frighteningly strong in order for us all to survive. For, after all, she was the one whom they left (and I don't hold this against them; I understand) with the children to raise, who had to *make* it somehow or the other. And we are still, so many of us, living that history.

"You would think that they would understand this, but few do. So it's up to us. We have got to understand them and save them for ourselves. How? By being, on one hand, persons in our own right and, on the other, fully the woman and the wife. . . . Christ, listen to who's talking! I had my chance. And I tried. Very hard. But it wasn't enough."

The festive sounds of the wake had died to a sober murmur beyond the bedroom. The crowd had gone, leaving only Reena and myself upstairs and the last of Aunt Vi's closest friends in the basement below. They were drinking coffee. I smelled it, felt its warmth and intimacy in the empty house, heard the distant tapping of the cups against the saucers and voices muted by grief. The wake had come full circle: they were again mourning Aunt Vi.

And Reena might have been mourning with them, sitting there amid the satin roses, framed by the massive headboard. Her hands lay as if they had been broken in her lap. Her eyes were like those of someone blind or dead. I got up to go and get some coffee for her.

"You met my husband," she said quickly, stopping me.

"Have I?" I said, sitting down again.

"Yes, before we were married even. At an autograph party for you. He was free-lancing—he's a photographer—and one of the Negro magazines had sent him to cover the party."

As she went on to describe him I remembered him vaguely, not his face, but his rather large body stretching and bending with a dancer's fluidity and grace as he took the pictures. I had heard him talking to a group of people about some issue on race relations very much in the news then and had been struck by his vehemence. For the moment I had found this almost odd, since he was so fair-skinned he could have passed for white.

They had met, Reena told me now, at a benefit show for a Harlem day nursery given by one of the progressive groups she belonged to, and had married a month afterward. From all that she said they had had a full and exciting life for a long time. Her words were so vivid that I could almost see them: she with her startling blackness and extraordinary force and he with his near-white skin and a militancy which matched hers; both of them moving among the disaffected in New York, their stand on political and social issues equally uncompromising, the line of their allegiance reaching directly to all those trapped in Harlem. And they had lived the meaning of this allegiance, so that even when they could have afforded a life among the black bourgeoisie of St. Albans or Teaneck, they had chosen to live if not in Harlem so close that there was no difference.

"I—we—were so happy I was frightened at times. Not that anything would change between us, but that someone or something in the world outside us would invade our private place and destroy us out of envy. Perhaps this is what did happen. . . ." She shrugged and even tried to smile but she could not manage it. "Something slipped in while we weren't looking and began its deadly work.

"Maybe it started when Dave took a job with a Negro magazine. I'm not sure. Anyway, in no time, he hated it: the routine, unimaginative pictures he had to take and the magazine itself, which dealt only in unrealities: the high-society world of the black bourgeoisie and the spectacular strides Negroes were making in all fields—you know the type. Yet Dave wouldn't leave. It wasn't the money, but a kind of safety which he had never experienced before which kept him there. He would talk about free-lancing again, about storming the gates of the white magazines downtown, of opening his own studio—but he never acted on any one of these things. You see, despite his talent— and he was very talented—he had a diffidence that was fatal.

"When I understood this I literally forced him to open the studio—and perhaps I should have been more subtle and indirect, but that's not my nature. Besides, I was frightened and desperate to help. Nothing happened for a time. Dave's work was too experimental to be commercial. Gradually, though, his photographs started appearing in the prestige camera magazines and money from various awards and exhibits and an occasional assignment started coming in.

"This wasn't enough somehow. Dave also wanted the big, gaudy commercial success that would dazzle and confound that white world downtown and force it to *see* him. And yet, as I said before, he couldn't bring himself to try— and this contradiction began to get to him after awhile.

"It was then, I think, that I began to fail him. I didn't know how to help, you see. I had never felt so inadequate before. And this was very strange and disturbing for someone like me. I was being submerged in his problems—and I began fighting against this.

"I started working again (I had stopped after the second baby). And I was lucky because I got back my old job. And unlucky because Dave saw it as my way of pointing up his deficiencies. I couldn't convince him otherwise: that I had to do it for my own sanity. He would accuse me of wanting to see him fail, of trapping him in all kinds of responsibilities. . . . After a time we both got caught up in this thing, an ugliness came between us, and I began to answer his anger with anger and to trade him insult for insult.

"Things fell apart very quickly after that. I couldn't bear the pain of living with him—the insults, our mutual despair, his mocking, the silence. I couldn't subject the children to it any longer. The divorce didn't take long. And thank God, because of the children, we are pleasant when we have to see each other. He's making out very well, I hear."

She said nothing more, but simply bowed her head as though waiting for me to pass judgment on her. I don't know how long we remained like this, but when Reena finally raised her head, the darkness at the window had vanished and dawn was a still, gray smoke against the pane.

"Do you know," she said, and her eyes were clear and a smile had won out over pain, "I enjoy being alone. I don't tell people this because they'll accuse me of either lying or deluding myself. But I do. Perhaps, as my mother tells me, it's only temporary. I don't think so, though. I feel I don't ever want to be involved again. It's not that I've lost interest in men. I go out occasionally, but it's never anything serious. You see, I have all that I want for now."

Her children first of all, she told me, and from her description they sounded intelligent and capable. She was a friend as well as a mother to them, it seemed. They were planning, the four of them, to spend the summer touring Canada. "I will feel that I have done well by them if I give them, if nothing more, a sense of themselves and their worth and importance as black people. Everything I do with them, for them, is to this end. I don't want them ever to be confused about this. They must have their identifications straight from the beginning. No white dolls for them!"

Then her job. She was working now as a researcher for a small progressive news magazine with the promise that once she completed her master's in journalism (she was working on the thesis now) she might get a chance to do some minor reporting. And like most people, she hoped to write someday. "If I can ever stop talking away my substance," she said laughing.

And she was still active in any number of social-action groups. In another week or so she would be heading a delegation of mothers down to City Hall "to give the mayor a little hell about conditions in the schools in Harlem." She had started an organization that was carrying on an almost door-to-door campaign in her neighborhood to expose, as she put it, "the blood suckers: all those slumlords and storekeepers with their fixed scales, the finance companies that never tell you the real price of a thing, the petty salesmen that leech off the poor. . . ." In May she was taking her two older girls on a nationwide pilgrimage to Washington to urge for a more rapid implementation of the school-desegregation law.

"It's uncanny," she said, and the laugh which accompanied the words was warm, soft with wonder at herself, girlish even, and the air in the room which had refused her laughter before rushed to absorb this now. "Really uncanny. Here I am, practically middle-aged, with three children to raise by myself and with little or no money to do it, and yet I feel, strangely enough, as though life is just beginning—that it's new and fresh with all kinds of possibilities. Maybe it's because I've been through my purgatory and I can't ever be overwhelmed again. I don't know. Anyway, you should see me on evenings after I put the children to bed. I sit alone in the living room (I've repainted it and changed all the furniture since Dave's gone, so that it would at least look different)—I sit there making plans and all of them seem possible. The most important plan right now is Africa. I've already started saving the fare."

I asked her whether she was planning to live there permanently and she said simply, "I want to live and work there. For how long, for a lifetime, I can't say. All I know is that I have to. For myself and for my children. It is important that they see black people who have truly a place and history of their own and who are building for a new and, hopefully, more sensible world. And I must see it, get close to it, because I can never lose the sense of being a displaced person here in America because of my color. Oh, I know I should remain and fight not only for integration (even though, frankly, I question whether I want to be integrated into America as it stands now, with its complacency and materialism, its soullessness) but to help change the country into something better, sounder—if that is still possible. But I have to go to Africa. . . .

"Poor Aunt Vi," she said after a long silence and straightened one of the roses she had crushed. "She never really got to enjoy her bed of roses what with only Thursdays and every other Sunday off. All that hard work. All her life . . . Our lives have got to make more sense, if only for her."

We got up to leave shortly afterward. Reena was staying on to attend the burial, later in the morning, but I was taking the subway to Manhattan. We parted with the usual promise to get together and exchanged telephone numbers. And Reena did phone a week or so later. I don't remember what we talked about though.

Some months later I invited her to a party I was giving before leaving the country. But she did not come.

PAULE MARSHALL

Paule Marshall's parents immigrated to New York from Barbados shortly after World War I, and Ms. Marshall was born there (in Brooklyn) a decade later, April 9, 1929. After graduating Phi Beta Kappa from Brooklyn College in 1953, she worked as a journalist for *Our World* magazine from 1953 to 1956 and lectured in black literature at numerous colleges and universities. She has published two novels, *Brown Girl, Brownstones* (1959) and *The Chosen Place, the Timeless People* (1969), and a book of short stories, *Soul Clap Hands and Sing* (1961). A new novel in progress is tentatively entitled *Little Girl of All the Daughters*.

In her first novel, *Brown Girl, Brownstones,* the story of a Barbadian girl growing up in Brooklyn, Ms. Marshall captures the uniqueness of the Barbadian culture. In their language, for example, she sees irony and wit as well as a poetic skill with words and an ability for storytelling that are peculiarly Barbadian and, at their root, African. Through this language she is able to depict the rugged and determined sense of life that has enabled an exploited people to survive and even to transcend their oppression. Ms. Marshall continues to deal with the nature and effects of oppression in her second novel, *The Chosen Place, the Timeless People*. This novel uses a mythical Caribbean country to analyze the history of colonial oppression of Third World peoples.

Ms. Marshall sees the need to understand the past— both the historical and the personal past—as part of the

search for and the need for identity, questions that are of
vital importance for an oppressed people: "This personal
quest [for identity] became translated as I began to write,
into a belief that for black people to define ourselves on
our own terms we must consciously engage our past. . . .
this exploration of the past is vital in the work of con-
structing our future." Thus Selina Boyce, the young girl
in *Brown Girl, Brownstones,* rejects the materialism of
America and returns at the end of the book to the place of
her birth; Merle Kibona, in *The Chosen Place, the
Timeless People,* leaves her West Indian country and sets
out for Africa at the end of the book; and to complete the
trilogy, Ms. Marshall says the third and yet unfinished
novel will be concerned with Africa. Each character, then,
journeys both spiritually and physically through her history (as Reena does in the short story) to find for herself a
more truthful identity.

Reconciliation

A Sudden Trip Home in the Spring

ALICE WALKER

For the Wellesley Class

Sarah walked slowly off the tennis court, fingering the back of her head, feeling the sturdy dark hair that grew there. She was popular. As she walked along the path toward Talfinger Hall, her friends fell into place around her. They formed a warm, jostling group of six. Sarah, because she was taller than the rest, saw the messenger first.

"Miss Davis," he said, standing still until the group came abreast of him, "I've got a telegram for ye." Brian was Irish and always quite respectful. He stood with his cap in his hand until Sarah took the telegram. Then he gave a nod that included all the young ladies before he turned away. He was young and good-looking, though annoyingly servile, and Sarah's friends twittered.

"Well, open it!" someone cried, for Sarah stood staring at the yellow envelope, turning it over and over in her hand.

"Look at her," said one of the girls, "isn't she beautiful! Such eyes, and hair, and *skin!*"

Sarah's tall, caplike hair framed a face of soft brown angles, high cheekbones, and large, dark eyes. Her eyes enchanted her friends because they always seemed to know more, and to find more of life amusing, or sad, than Sarah cared to tell.

Her friends often teased Sarah about her beauty; they loved dragging her out of her room so that their boy friends, naïve and worldly young men from Princeton and Yale, could see her. They never guessed she found this distasteful. She was gentle with her friends, and her outrage at their tactlessness did not show. She was most often inclined to pity them, though embarrassment sometimes drove her to fraudulent expressions. Now she smiled and raised eyes and arms to heaven. She acknowledged their unearned curiosity as a mother endures the prying impatience of a child. Her friends beamed love and envy upon her as she tore open the telegram.

"He's dead," she said.

Her friends reached out for the telegram, their eyes on Sarah.

"It's her father," one of them said softly. "He died yesterday. Oh, Sarah," the girl whimpered, "I'm so sorry!"

"Me too." "So am I." "Is there anything we can do?"

But Sarah had walked away, head high and neck stiff.

"So graceful!" one of her friends said.

"Like a proud gazelle," said another. Then they all trooped to their dormitories to change for supper.

Talfinger Hall was a pleasant dorm. The common room just off the entrance had been made into a small modern-art gallery with some very good original paintings, lithographs, and collages. Pieces were constantly being stolen. Some of the girls could not resist an honest-to-God Chagall, signed (in the plate) by his own hand, though they could have afforded to purchase one from the gallery in town. Sarah Davis' room was next door to the gallery, but her walls were covered with inexpensive Gauguin reproductions, a Reubens ("The Head of a Negro"), a Modigliani, and a Picasso. There was a full wall of her own drawings, all of black women. She found black men impossible to draw or to paint; she could not bear to trace defeat onto blank pages. Her women figures were matronly, massive of arm, with a weary victory showing in their eyes. Surrounded by Sarah's drawings was a red SNCC poster of an old man holding a small girl whose face nestled in his shoulder. Sarah often felt she was the little girl whose face no one could see.

To leave Talfinger even for a few days filled Sarah with fear. Talfinger was her home now; it suited her better than any home she'd ever known. Perhaps she loved it because in winter there was a fragrant fireplace and snow outside her window. When hadn't she dreamed of fireplaces that really warmed, snow that almost pleasantly froze? Georgia seemed far away as she packed; she did not want to leave New York, where, her grandfather had liked to say, "the devil hangs out and catches young gals by the front of their dresses." He had always believed the South the best place to live on earth (never mind that certain people invariably marred the landscape), and swore he expected to die no more than a few miles from where he had been born. There was tenacity even in the gray frame house he lived in, and in scrawny animals on his farm who regularly reproduced. He was the first person Sarah wanted to see when she got home.

There was a knock on the door of the adjoining bathroom, and Sarah's suite mate entered, a loud Bach Concerto just finishing behind her. At first she stuck just her head into the room, but seeing Sarah fully dressed she trudged in and plopped down on the bed. She was a heavy blond girl with large, milk-white legs. Her eyes were small and her neck usually gray with grime.

"My, don't you look gorgeous," she said.

"Ah, Pam," said Sarah, waving her hand in disgust. In Georgia she knew that even to Pam she would be just another ordinarily attractive *colored* girl. In Georgia there were a million girls better looking. Pam wouldn't know that, of course, she'd never been to Georgia; she'd never even seen a black person to speak to—that is, before she met Sarah. One of her first poetic observations about Sarah was that she was "a poppy in a field of winter roses." She had found it weird that Sarah did not own more than one coat.

"Say, listen, Sarah," said Pam, "I heard about your father. I'm sorry. I really am."

"Thanks," said Sarah.

"Is there anything we can do? I thought, well, maybe you'd want my father to get somebody to fly you down. He'd go himself but he's taking mother to Madeira this week. You wouldn't have to worry about trains and things."

Pamela's father was one of the richest men in the world, though no one ever mentioned it. Pam only alluded to it at times of crisis, when a friend might benefit from the use of a private plane, train, or ship; or, if someone wanted to study the characteristics of a totally secluded village, island, or mountain, she might offer one of theirs. Sarah could not comprehend such wealth, and was always annoyed because Pam didn't look more like a billionaire's daughter. A billionaire's daughter, Sarah thought, should really be less horsy and brush her teeth more often.

"Gonna tell me what you're brooding about?" asked Pam.

Sarah stood in front of the radiator, her fingers resting on the window seat. Down below, girls were coming up the hill from supper.

"I'm thinking," she said, "of the child's duty to his parents after they are dead."

"Is that all?"

"Do you know," asked Sarah, "about Richard Wright and his father?"

Pamela frowned. Sarah looked down at her.

"Oh, I forgot," she said with a sigh, "they don't teach

Wright here. The poshest school in the U.S. and the girls come out ignorant." She looked at her watch, saw she had twenty minutes before her train. "Really," she said almost inaudibly, "why Tears Eliot, Ezratic Pound, and even Sara Teacake, and no Wright?" She and Pamela thought e. e. cummings very clever with his perceptive spelling of great literary names.

"Is he a poet, then?" asked Pam. She adored poetry, all poetry. Half of America's poetry she had, of course, not read, for the simple reason that she had never heard of it.

"No," said Sarah, "he wasn't a poet." She felt weary. "He was a man who wrote, a man who had trouble with his father." She began to walk about the room, and came to stand below the picture of the old man and the little girl.

"When he was a child," she continued, "his father ran off with another woman, and one day when Richard and his mother went to ask him for money to buy food, he laughingly rejected them. Richard, being very young, thought his father Godlike—big, omnipotent, unpredictable, undependable, and cruel; entirely in control of his universe; just like God. But, many years later, after Wright had become a famous writer, he went down to Mississippi to visit his father. He found, instead of God, just an old, watery-eyed field hand, bent from plowing, his teeth gone, smelling of manure. Richard realized that the most daring thing his 'God' had done was run off with that other woman."

"So?" asked Pam. "What 'duty' did he feel he owed the old man?"

"So," said Sarah, "that's what Wright wondered as he peered into that old, shifty-eyed Mississippi Negro face. What was the duty of the son of a destroyed man? The son of a man whose vision had stopped at the edge of fields that weren't even his. Who was Wright without his father? Was he Wright the great writer? Wright the Communist? Wright the French farmer? Wright whose wife could never accompany him to Mississippi? Was he, in fact, still his father's son? Or was he freed by his father's desertion to be nobody's son, to be his own father? Could he disavow his father and live? And if so, live as what? As whom? And for what purpose?"

"Well," said Pam, swinging her hair over her shoulders and squinting her small eyes, "if his father rejected him I don't see why Wright even bothered to go see him again. From what you've said, Wright earned the freedom to be whoever he wanted to be. To a strong man a father is not essential."

"Maybe not," said Sarah, "but Wright's father was one faulty door in a house of many ancient rooms. Was that one faulty door to shut him off forever from the rest of the house? That was the question. And though he answered this question eloquently in his work, where it really counted, one can only wonder if he was able to answer it satisfactorily—or at all—in his life."

"You're thinking of his father more as a symbol of something, aren't you?" asked Pam.

"I suppose," said Sarah, taking a last look around her room. "I see him as a door that refused to open, a hand that was always closed. A fist."

Pamela walked with her to one of the college limousines, and in a few minutes she was at the station. The train to the city was just arriving.

"Have a nice trip," said the middle-aged driver courteously as she took her suitcase from him. But, for about the thousandth time since she'd seen him, he winked at her.

Once away from her friends, she did not miss them. The school was all they had in common. How could they ever know her if they were not allowed to know Wright?

she wondered. She was interesting, "beautiful," only because they had no idea what made her, charming only because they had no idea from where she came. And where they came from, though she glimpsed it—in themselves and in F. Scott Fitzgerald—she was never to enter. She hadn't the inclination or the proper ticket.

II

Her father's body was in Sarah's old room. The bed had been taken down to make room for the flowers and chairs and casket. Sarah looked for a long time into the face, as if to find some answer to her questions written there. It was the same face, a dark, Shakespearean head framed by gray, woolly hair and split almost in half by a short, gray mustache. It was a completely silent face, a shut face. But her father's face also looked fat, stuffed, and ready to burst. He wore a navy-blue suit, white shirt, and black tie. Sarah bent and loosened the tie. Tears started behind her shoulder blades but did not reach her eyes.

"There's a rat here under the casket," she called to her brother, who apparently did not hear her, for he did not come in. She was alone with her father, as she had rarely been when he was alive. When he was alive she had avoided him.

"Where's that girl at?" her father would ask. "Done closed herself up in her room again," he would answer himself.

For Sarah's mother had died in her sleep one night. Just gone to bed tired and never got up. And Sarah had blamed her father.

Stare the rat down, thought Sarah; surely that will help. *Perhaps it doesn't matter whether I misunderstood or never understood.*

"We moved so much, looking for crops, a place to *live,*" her father had moaned, accompanied by Sarah's stony silence. "The moving killed her. And now we have a real house, with *four* rooms, and a mailbox on the *porch*, and it's too late. She gone. *She* ain't here to see it." On very bad days her father would not eat at all. At night he did not sleep.

Whatever had made her think she knew what love was or was not?

Here she was, Sarah Davis, immersed in Camusian philosophy, versed in many languages, a poppy, of all things, among winter roses. But before she became a poppy she was a native Georgian sunflower, but still had not spoken the language they both knew. Not to him.

Stare the rat down, she thought, and did. The rascal dropped his bold eyes and slunk away. Sarah felt she had, at least, accomplished something.

Why did she have to see the picture of her mother, the one on the mantel among all the religious doodads, come to life? Her mother had stood stout against the years, clean gray braids shining across the top of her head, her eyes snapping, protective. Talking to her father.

"He called you out your name, we'll leave this place today. Not tomorrow. That be too late. Today!" Her mother was magnificent in her quick decisions.

"But what about your garden, the children, the change of schools?" Her father would be holding, most likely, the wide brim of his hat in nervously twisting fingers.

"He called you out your name, we go!"

And go they would. Who knew exactly where, before they moved? Another soundless place, walls falling down, roofing gone; another face to please without leaving too much of her father's pride at his feet. But to Sarah then, no matter with what alacrity her father moved, foot-dragging alone was visible.

The moving killed her, her father had said, but the moving was also love.

Did it matter now that often he had threatened their lives with the rage of his despair? That once he had spanked the crying baby violently, who later died of something else altogether . . . and that the next day they moved?

"No," said Sarah aloud, "I don't think it does."

"Huh?" It was her brother, tall, wiry, black, deceptively calm. As a child he'd had an irrepressible temper. As a grown man he was tensely smooth, like a river that any day will overflow its bed.

He had chosen a dull gray casket. Sarah wished for red. Was it Dylan Thomas who had said something grand about the dead offering "deep, dark defiance"? It didn't matter; there were more ways to offer defiance than with a red casket.

"I was just thinking," said Sarah, "that with us Mama and Daddy were saying NO with capital letters."

"I don't follow you," said her brother. He had always been the activist in the family. He simply directed his calm rage against any obstacle that might exist, and awaited the consequences with the same serenity he awaited his sister's answer. Not for him the philosophical confusions and poetic observations that hung his sister up.

"That's because you're a radical preacher," said Sarah, smiling up at him. "You deliver your messages in person with your own body." It excited her that her brother had at last imbued their childhood Sunday sermons with the reality of fighting for change. And saddened her that no matter how she looked at it this seemed more important than Medieval Art, Course 201.

III

"Yes, Grandma," Sarah replied. "Cresselton is for girls only, and *No*, Grandma, I am not pregnant."

Her grandmother stood clutching the broad, wooden

handle of her black bag, which she held, with elbows bent, in front of her stomach. Her eyes glinted through round, wire-framed glasses. She spat into the grass outside the privy. She had insisted that Sarah accompany her to the toilet while the body was being taken into the church. She had leaned heavily on Sarah's arm, her own arm thin and the flesh like crepe.

"I guess they teach you how to really handle the world," she said. "And who knows, the Lord is everywhere. I would like a whole lot to see a great-grand. You don't specially have to be married, you know. That's why I felt free to ask." She reached into her bag and took out a Three Sixes bottle, which she proceeded to drink from, taking deep, swift swallows with her head thrown back.

"There are very few black boys near Cresselton," Sarah explained, watching the corn liquor leave the bottle in spurts and bubbles. "Besides, I'm really caught up now in my painting and sculpturing . . ." Should she mention how much she admired Giacometti's work? No, she decided. Even if her grandmother had heard of him, and Sarah was positive she had not, she would surely think his statues much too thin. This made Sarah smile and remember how difficult it had been to convince her grandmother that even if Cresselton had not given her a scholarship she would have managed to go there anyway. Why? Because she wanted somebody to teach her to paint and to sculpture, and Cresselton had the best teachers. Her grandmother's notion of a successful granddaughter was a married one, pregnant the first year.

"Well," said her grandmother, placing the bottle with dignity back into her purse and gazing pleadingly into Sarah's face, "I sure would 'preshate a great-grand." Seeing her granddaughter's smile, she heaved a great sigh, and, walking rather haughtily over the stones and grass, made her way to the church steps.

As they walked down the aisle, Sarah's eyes rested on the back of her grandfather's head. He was sitting on the front middle bench in front of the casket, his hair extravagantly long and white and softly kinked. When she sat down beside him, her grandmother sitting next to him on the other side, he turned toward her and gently took her hand in his. Sarah briefly leaned her cheek against his shoulder and felt like a child again.

IV

They had come twenty miles from town, on a dirt road, and the hot spring sun had drawn a steady rich scent from the honeysuckle vines along the way. The church was a bare, weatherbeaten ghost of a building with hollow windows and a sagging door. Arsonists had once burned it to the ground, lighting the dry wood of the walls with the flames from the crosses they carried. The tall, spreading red-oak tree under which Sarah had played as a child still dominated the churchyard, stretching its branches widely from the roof of the church to the other side of the road.

After a short and eminently dignified service, during which Sarah and her grandfather alone did not cry, her father's casket was slid into the waiting hearse and taken the short distance to the cemetery, an overgrown wilderness whose stark white stones appeared to be the small ruins of an ancient civilization. There Sarah watched her grandfather from the corner of her eye. He did not seem to bend under the grief of burying a son. His back was straight, his eyes dry and clear. He was simply and solemnly heroic, a man who kept with pride his family's trust and his own grief. *It is strange,* Sarah thought, *that I never thought to paint him like this, simply as he stands; without anonymous, meaningless people hovering beyond his profile; his face turned proud and brownly against the light.* The defeat that had frightened her in the faces of black men was the defeat of black forever defined by white. But that defeat was nowhere on her grandfather's face. He stood like a rock, outwardly calm, the grand patriarch of the Davis family. The family alone defined him, and he was not about to let them down.

"One day I will paint you, Grandpa," she said as they turned to go. "Just as you stand here now, with just," she moved closer and touched his face with her hand, "just the right stubborn tenseness of your cheek. Just that look of Yes and No in your eyes."

"You wouldn't want to paint an old man like me," he said, looking deep into her eyes from wherever his mind had been. "If you want to make me, make me up in stone."

The completed grave was plump and red. The wreaths of flowers were arranged all on one side, so that from the road there appeared to be only a large mass of flowers. But already the wind was tugging at the rose petals and the rain was making dabs of faded color all over the green-foam frames. In a week, the displaced honeysuckle vines, the wild roses, the grapevines, the grass, would be back. Nothing would seem to have changed.

V

"What do you mean, come *home?*" Her brother seemed genuinely amused. "We're all proud of you. How many black girls are at that school? Just *you?* Well, just one more besides you, and she's from the North. That's really something!"

"I'm glad you're pleased," said Sarah.

"Pleased! Why, it's what Mama would have wanted, a good education for little Sarah; and what Dad would have wanted too, if he could have wanted anything after Mama died. You were always smart. When you were two and I was five you showed me how to eat ice cream without get-

ting it all over me. First, you said, nip off the bottom of
the cone with your teeth, and suck the ice cream down. I
never knew *how* you were supposed to eat the stuff once it
began to melt."

"I don't know," she said; "sometimes you can want
something a whole lot, only to find out later that it wasn't
what you *needed* at all."

Sarah shook her head, a frown coming between her
eyes. "I sometimes spend *weeks*," she said, "trying to
sketch or paint a face that is unlike every other face
around me, except, vaguely, for one. Can I help but
wonder if I'm in the right place?"

Her brother smiled. "You mean to tell me you spend
weeks trying to draw one face, and you still wonder
whether you're in the right place? You must be kidding!"
He chucked her under the chin and laughed out loud.
"You learn how to draw the face," he said, "then you
learn how to paint me and how to make Grandpa up in
stone. Then you can come home or go live in Paris,
France. It'll be the same thing."

It was the unpreacher-like gaiety of his affection that
made her cry. She leaned peacefully into her brother's
arms. She wondered if Richard Wright had had a brother.

"You are my door to all the rooms," she said; "don't ever
close."

And he said, "I won't," as if he understood what she
meant.

VI

"When will we see you again, young woman?" he
asked later as he drove her to the bus stop.

"I'll sneak up one day and surprise you," she said.

At the bus stop, in front of a tiny service station, Sarah
hugged her brother with all her strength. The white sta-

tion attendant stopped his work to leer at them, his eyes bold and careless.

"Did you ever think," said Sarah, "that we are a very old people in a very young place?"

She watched her brother from a window on the bus; her eyes did not leave his face until the little station was out of sight and the big Greyhound lurched on its way toward Atlanta. She would fly from there to New York.

VII

She took the train to the campus.

"My," said one of her friends, "you look wonderful! Home sure must agree with you!"

"Sarah was home?" someone who didn't know asked. "Oh, *great,* how was it?"

Well, how was it? went an echo in Sarah's head. The noise of the echo almost made her dizzy.

"How was it?" she asked aloud, searching for, and regaining, her balance.

"How was it?" She watched her reflection in a pair of smiling hazel eyes.

"It was fine," she said slowly, returning the smile, thinking of her grandfather. "Just fine."

The girl's smile deepened. Sarah watched her swinging along toward the back tennis courts, hair blowing in the wind.

Stare the rat down, thought Sarah; *and whether it disappears or not, I am a woman in the world. I have buried my father, and shall soon know how to make my grandpa up in stone.*

Selected Bibliography

ALICE WALKER

Books

Once. New York: Harcourt, Brace & World, 1968. (Poetry)

The Third Life of Grange Copeland. New York: Harcourt Brace Jovanovich, 1970. (Novel)

Revolutionary Petunias. New York: Harcourt Brace Jovanovich, 1973. (Poetry)

Langston Hughes. New York: Thomas Y. Crowell, 1974. (Biography for young children)

In Love & Trouble: Stories of Black Women. New York: Harcourt Brace Jovanovich, 1974. (Short stories)

Articles

"But Yet and Still, the Cotton Gin Kept on Working," *The Black Scholar,* Jan.–Feb. 1970.

"The Black Writer and the Southern Experience," *New South,* Fall 1970.

"The Unglamorous but Worthwhile Duties of the Black Revolutionary Artist, or of the Black Writer Who Simply Works and Writes," *The Black Collegian,* October 1971.

"Women on Women," panel discussion with Lillian Hellman et al., *The American Scholar,* Fall 1972.

"Something to Do with Real Life," interview with Eudora Welty, *Harvard Advocate,* Winter 1973.

"Interview." In: *Interviews with Black Writers,* by John O'Brien (New York: Liveright, 1973).

"Judith Jamison Dances 'Cry,'" an essay-poem, *Ms.,* I (May 1973).

"In Search of Our Mothers' Gardens," *Ms.,* II (May 1974).

"In Search of Zora Neale Hurston," *Ms.,* III (March 1975).

"Staying at Home in Mississippi," New York *Times Magazine*, August 26, 1973.

Poems (uncollected)

"Janie Crawford," *Aphra*, 5 (Fall 1974).

"Early Losses: A Requiem," *New Letters*, 41 (Winter 1974).

"In These Dissenting Times," *Black World*, November 1970.

Short Stories (uncollected)

"A Sudden Trip Home in the Spring," *Essence*, September 1971.

"The First Day (A Fable After Brown)," *Freedomways*, 14 (Fourth Quarter 1974).

Criticism

Callahan, John. "The Higher Ground of Alice Walker," *The New Republic*, September 14, 1974, pp. 21–22.

Coles, Robert. "To Try Men's Souls," *The New Yorker*, February 27, 1971, pp. 104–6.

Fowler, Carolyn. "Solid at the Core." *Freedomways*, 14 (First Quarter 1974), pp. 59–62.

Hairston, Loyle. "Work of Rare Beauty and Power." *Freedomways*, 11 (Second Quarter 1971), pp. 170–77.

Schorer, Mark. "Novels and Nothingness," *American Scholar*, Winter 1970–71, pp. 169–70.

Smith, Barbara. "The Souls of Black Women." *Ms.*, II (February 1974), pp. 42–43, 78.

Ward, Jerry. Review of *Revolutionary Petunias*, CLA *Journal*, 17 (September 1973), pp. 127–29.

Washington, Mary Helen. Review of *Revolutionary Petunias*, *Black World*, 22 (September 1973), pp. 51–52, 89.

———. Review of *In Love and Trouble*, *Black World*, 23 (October 1974), pp. 51–52.

———. "Black Women Myth and Image Makers," *Black World*, 23 (August 1974), pp. 10–18.

JEAN WHEELER SMITH

Stories

"That She Would Dance No More," *Negro Digest*, 17 (January 1967), pp. 59–68.

"The Machine," *Negro Digest*, 17 (November 1967), pp. 60–74.

"Somethin-to-Eat," *Black World*, 20 (June 1971), pp. 70–76.

"Frankie Mae." In: *Black Short Story Anthology*, ed. by Woodie King (New York: Signet, 1972).

Plays

O.C.'s Heart, Negro Digest, 19 (April 1970), pp. 56–76.

Articles

"I Learned to Feel Black." In: *The Black Power Revolt*, ed. by Floyd B. Barbour (Boston: Porter Sargent, 1968).

GWENDOLYN BROOKS

Poetry

A Street in Bronzeville. New York: Harper & Brothers, 1945.

Annie Allen. New York: Harper & Brothers, 1949.

Bronzeville Boys and Girls. New York: Harper & Brothers, 1956.

The Bean Eaters. New York: Harper & Row, 1960.

Selected Poems. New York: Harper & Row, 1963.

In the Mecca. New York: Harper & Row, 1968.

Riot. Detroit: Broadside Press, 1971.

A Broadside Treasury (ed.). Detroit: Broadside Press, 1971.

Family Pictures. Detroit: Broadside Press, 1971.

Jump Bad: A New Chicago Anthology (ed.). Detroit: Broadside Press, 1971.

The World of Gwendolyn Brooks (includes: *A Street in Bronzeville, Annie Allen, Maud Martha, The Bean Eaters, In the Mecca*). New York: Harper & Row, 1971.

Prose

Maud Martha. New York: Harper & Brothers, 1953. (Novel)

The Black Position (ed.). Detroit: Broadside Press, 1971. (An annual periodical)

Report from Part One: An Autobiography. Detroit: Broadside Press, 1972.

Articles

"Why Negro Women Leave Home," *Negro Digest,* March 1951, pp. 26–28.

"Forward." In: *New Negro Poets, U.S.A.,* ed. by Langston Hughes (Bloomington: Indiana University Press, 1964).

"Autobiographical Excerpt: Report from Part One," *Black World,* September 1972, pp. 4–12.

"A Report from: *Report from Part One,*" *Ebony,* March 1973, pp. 116–20.

"Introduction." In: *The Poetry of Black America: Anthology of the 20th Century,* ed. by Arnold Adoff (New York: Harper & Row, 1973).

Bibliographies

Loff, Jon N. "Gwendolyn Brooks: A Bibliography," *CLA Journal,* 17 (September 1973), pp. 21–32.

Williams, Ora. *American Black Women in the Arts and Sciences: A Bibliographic Survey.* Metuchen, N.J.: Scarecrow Press, 1973, pp. 59–61.

Criticism

Barksdale, Richard; and Kinnamon, Keneth; (eds.). *Black Writers of America: A Comprehensive Anthology.* New York: Macmillan, 1972, pp. 712–22.

Baker, Houston A. "The Achievement of Gwendolyn

Brooks," *CLA Journal*, 16 (September 1972), pp. 23–31.

Crockett, Jacqueline. "An Essay on Gwendolyn Brooks," *Negro History Bulletin*, 19 (November 1955), pp. 37–39.

Davis, Arthur P. "The Black-and-Tan Motif in the Poetry of Gwendolyn Brooks," *CLA Journal*, 6 (December 1962), pp. 90–97.

Furman, Marva Riley. "Gwendolyn Brooks: The 'Unconditioned' Poet," *CLA Journal*, 17 (September 1973), pp. 1–10.

Hansell, William H. "Aestheticism Versus Political Militancy in Gwendolyn Brooks's 'The Chicago Picasso' and 'The Wall,'" *CLA Journal*, 17 (September 1973), pp. 11–15.

Hudson, Clenora. "Racial Themes in the Poetry of Gwendolyn Brooks," *CLA Journal*, 17 (September 1973), pp. 16–20.

Kent, George. "The Poetry of Gwendolyn Brooks: Part I," *Black World*, September 1971, pp. 30–43.

———. "The Poetry of Gwendolyn Brooks: Part II," *Black World*, October 1971, pp. 36–48, passim.

Lewis, Ida. "Conversation: Gwen Brooks and Ida Lewis," *Essence*, April 1971, pp. 27–31.

Lee, Don L. "The Achievement of Gwendolyn Brooks," *The Black Scholar*, 3 (Summer 1972), pp. 32–41.

Washington, Mary Helen. Review of *Report from Part One*, *Black World* (March 1973), pp. 51–52, passim.

LOUISE MERIWETHER

Books

Daddy Was a Number Runner. Englewood Cliffs, N.J.: Prentice-Hall, 1970. (Novel)

The Freedom Ship of Robert Smalls. Englewood Cliffs, N.J.: Prentice-Hall, 1971. (Children's book)

The Heart Man: Dr. Daniel Hale Williams. Englewood Cliffs, N.J.: Prentice-Hall, 1972. (Children's book)

Don't Take the Bus on Monday: The Rosa Parks Story.

Englewood Cliffs, N.J.: Prentice-Hall, 1973. (Children's book)

Short Stories

"Daddy Was a Number Runner," *Antioch Review*, Fall Quarter 1967.

"The Thick End Is for Whipping," *Negro Digest*, 18 (November 1968), pp. 55–62.

"A Happening in Barbados," *Antioch Review*, 28 (Spring 1968).

"That Girl from Creektown." In: *Black Review No. 2*, ed. by Mel Watkins (New York: William Morrow, 1972), pp. 79–92.

Articles

"Profile on Judge Vanio Spencer," *Sepia*, March 1962.

"Profile on Leontyne King," *Sepia*, June 1962.

"Profile on Attorney Audrey Boswell Jones," *Sepia*, July 1962.

"The Quickening Pace of Negro Politics," *Sepia*, April 1963.

"America Applauds Grace Bumbry," *Sepia*, June 1963.

"James Baldwin: Fiery Voice of the Negro Revolt," *Negro Digest*, August 1963.

"No Race Pride," *Bronze America*, June 1964.

"The Negro Who Discovered the North Pole," *Bronze America*, August 1964.

"America's Number One Newspaper Woman," *Bronze America*, August 1964.

"The Amen Corner," *Negro Digest*, January 1965.

"The Negro: Half a Man in a White World," *Negro Digest*, October 1965.

"What They Say in Watts," *Frontier*, October 1965.

"The New Face of History," *Frontier*, November 1965.

"Black Man, Do You Love Me?" *Essence*, May 1970.

Criticism

Giovanni, Nikki. Review of *Daddy Was a Number Runner*, *Black World*, 19 (July 1970), pp. 85–86.

King, Helen. Review of *Daddy Was a Number Runner*, *Black World*, 19 (May 1970), pp. 51–52.

Marshall, Paule. Review of *Daddy Was a Number Runner*, New York *Times Book Review*, June 28, 1970, p. 31.

TONI MORRISON

Books

The Bluest Eye. New York: Holt, Rinehart & Winston, 1970. (Novel)

Sula. New York: Alfred A. Knopf, 1974. (Novel)

Articles

"What the Black Woman Thinks About Women's Lib," New York *Times Magazine*, August 22, 1971.

"Behind the Making of *The Black Book*," *Black World*, 23 (February 1974), pp. 86–90.

"Rediscovering Black History," New York *Times Magazine*, August 11, 1974.

PAULE MARSHALL

Books

Brown Girl, Brownstones. New York: Random House, 1959. (Novel)

Soul Clap Hands and Sing. New York: Atheneum, 1961. (Short stories)

The Chosen Place, the Timeless People. New York: Harcourt, Brace & World, 1969. (Novel)

Short Stories

"Reena." In: *American Negro Short Stories*, ed. by John Henrik Clarke (New York: Hill & Wang, 1966).

"Some Get Wasted." In: *Harlem, U.S.A.*, ed. and with an introduction by John Henrik Clarke (Berlin: Seven Seas, 1964).

"To Da-duh in Memoriam." In: *Black Voices*, ed. by Abraham Chapman (New York: Mentor, 1968).

Articles

"The Negro Woman in American Literature" (speech at the Harlem Writers' Guild Conference, New York City, Spring 1965), *Freedomways*, 6 (Winter 1966), pp. 20–25.

"Shaping the World of My Art," *New Letters*, 40 (Autumn 1973), pp. 97–112.

Biography and Criticism

Barksdale, Richard; and Kinnamon, Keneth; (eds.). *Black Writers of America: A Comprehensive Anthology*. New York: Macmillan, 1972, pp. 773–81.

Kapai, Seela. "Dominant Themes and Techniques in Paule Marshall's Fiction," *CLA Journal*, 16 (September 1972), pp. 49–59.

Miller, Adam David. Review of *Brown Girl, Brownstones*, *The Black Scholar*, 3 (May 1972), pp. 56–58.

Nazareth, Peter. "Paule Marshall's Timeless People," *New Letters*, 40 (Autumn 1973), pp. 116–31.

Stoelting, Winifred L. "Time Past and Time Present: The Search for Viable Links in *The Chosen Place, the Timeless People*," *CLA Journal*, 16 (September 1972), pp. 60–71.

Williams, Ora. *American Black Women in the Arts and Sciences: A Bibliographic Survey*. Metuchen, N.J.: Scarecrow Press, 1973.

TONI CADE BAMBARA

Books

The Black Woman (ed.). New York: New American Library, 1970. (Anthology)

Tales and Stories for Black Folks (ed.). New York: Doubleday, 1971. (Anthology)

Gorilla, My Love. New York: Random House, 1972. (Short stories)

Articles

"Black Theater." In: *Black Expression,* ed. by Addison Gayle (New York: Weybright & Talley, 1969).

"On the Issue of Roles." In: *The Black Woman,* ed. by Toni Cade (New York: New American Library, 1970).

"The Pill: Genocide or Liberation?" In: *The Black Woman,* ed. by Toni Cade (New York: New American Library, 1970).

"Black Theatre of the 60's." In: *Backgrounds to Blackamerican Literature,* ed. by Ruth Miller (London: Chandler, 1971).

"Black Man/Black Woman," *Essence,* October 1973, p. 37 and passim.